Pyro
<u>Marketing</u>

Pyro
Marketing

*The Four-Step Strategy to
Ignite Customer Evangelists
and Keep Them for Life*

Greg Stielstra

HarperBusiness

An Imprint of HarperCollinsPublishers

FIRST EDITION

Designed by Nancy Singer Olaguera
Illustrations by Brook Wainwright

Library of Congress Cataloging-in-Publication Data has been applied for.

ISBN 0-06-077670-6

05 06 07 08 09 ISPN/RRD 10 9 8 7 6 5 4 3 2 1

To every businessperson who has ever
thought there must be a better way to
market your products or services, may
you have now the vision to see it and the
courage to see it through.

Contents

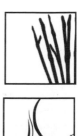

Acknowledgments

Noticing my sullen mood one day when I was ten, my mother asked what was wrong. "There is nothing left to invent," I complained. "Other people have already thought of everything." My mother laughed because she knew otherwise.

If new ideas do come, they often die for lack of a sponsor. I owe a debt of gratitude, therefore, to my publisher Steve Hanselman. He took a chance on a new idea by an unproven author. Steve believed in PyroMarketing and he believed in me and you would not be holding this book were it not for his vision and courage.

Thanks to my editor Herb Schaffner for his patience, his kindness, and for the myriad ways he improved my manuscript.

Many thanks to Rick Warren and the staff at Saddleback Church for allowing me to describe the plan they used to touch millions of lives and make *The Purpose-Driven® Life* the best-selling hardcover in American history. I am honored to have played a supporting role.

In the chapter titled "Fan the Flames," I drew heavily on the work of Duncan J. Watts who, in his brilliant book *Six Degrees*, buttressed my intuition with science. I am humbled by both his intellect and skill as a writer. If you are intrigued at all by my simple description, I encourage you to read his wonderful work.

Thanks as well to Arthur M. Hughes. I spend a chapter exploring the importance of consumer databases, Arthur has spent his entire career. You will benefit from reading his book *Strategic Database Marketing*. I certainly did.

I want to thank my friends at Zondervan and the Westar Media Group for their many contributions to this project. They gave me time to write and promote this book. They trudged through early writing samples and improved them with their smart advice. Most of all, they put up with me and my nonstop chatter about fire and marketing.

Special thanks as well to Michael Ranville, Kurt Dietsch, and all of the wonderful people at DDM Marketing Communications. They understand PyroMarketing and employ its principles better than any agency with which I've previously worked. They built www.pyromarketing.com and have helped promote my book in so many ways. If you embrace PyroMarketing and need an agency please visit www.ddmnet.com.

I owe the greatest thanks to my family, my wife Amy and children Dominic, Shelby, and Darby Sue, my mother and father and sisters and brother for they have sacrificed the most. I had no idea when I began writing that this book would cause me to be, either absent, or present but distracted, for the better part of a year. For missing me when I was gone and tolerating me when I was present I love and thank you all.

And finally I thank almighty God, the creator of fire and the giver of ideas, for saving one for me.

Introduction

MARKETING IS FIRE

The best way to understand marketing, the way its messages are sent, received, acted upon and spread, is to think of it as fire. Water metaphors that encouraged marketers to saturate consumers with a flood of messages are washed up. More recent attempts to explain the process by comparing marketing to contagion or guerrilla warfare are incomplete. Pyro-Marketing, however, is more than simply a new metaphor; it describes an entirely new way to think about marketing. The recent presidential election, major motion pictures, and best-selling books illustrate its success. This book describes its principles—principles that are dramatically different from the mass marketing approach they replace.

Mass marketing emerged from the economy of the mid–twentieth century as an effective way to promote products. It was a simpler time. A smaller selection of products competed for consumers' money. A smaller number of advertisements, delivered by many fewer media outlets, vied for their attention. People's perceptual capacity easily handled the load. People noticed advertising, eagerly processed its messages, and considered each offer. Advertising worked. And because it worked, it was quickly overworked. The key, it seemed, to increased sales was increased advertising. The more people were exposed to advertising, the more they bought. The two were linked. The relationship seemed causal. Business quickly noticed the connection and, in its quest to turn up sales, has been turning up advertising ever since.

Mass advertising's effectiveness, however, has been deteriorating since reaching its heyday in the late 1960s. Today, much of it inundates and annoys disinterested people with irrelevant messages.

TOO MUCH

Advertising is everywhere. It clogs e-mail in-boxes; it's stuck to supermarket floors; it's on movie theater screens, on gas pumps, and even adorns restroom walls. Yesterday you were exposed to 3,000 advertisements. Today you will be exposed to 3,000 more. Can you name them all? Could you list 300? Are you able to recall 30, or even 3?

The increase in ads as a "solution" for their decreased effectiveness has actually worsened the problem. The resulting deluge of advertising has saturated the market, but it hasn't improved results. The opposite is true. The rising tide of advertising has fostered growing resistance and negativity among those it targets. Consumers are drowning.

A recent Yankelovich survey found that 65 percent of Americans feel "constantly bombarded with too much marketing and advertising." Sixty-one percent feel the volume of advertising is out of control, while 69 percent are interested in devices that skip or block advertising messages. These attitudes represent more than a lack of effectiveness; they reveal a powerful consumer backlash against this century-long torrent of advertising.

Sixty percent of consumers confess to having a much more negative opinion of marketing and advertising than they did a few years ago, the Yankelovich survey found, while 50 percent actually avoid buying products that overwhelm them with advertising. Astonishingly, a third of all Americans would be willing to accept a slightly lower standard of living to live in a society without advertising. More than a failure to sell, advertising is actually repelling the very people it was supposed to attract. What's a marketer to do?

SPARKING AN IDEA

I was depressed by those sobering statistics. I knew traditional mass marketing had lost its sting and that consumers were increasingly wary and resistant but I couldn't use that as an excuse. As the senior marketing director for the Trade Book Group at Zondervan, the world's leading Christian publisher, I had books to sell. And while my experience had confirmed that most of what posed as advertising didn't work, it also proved that some did. Sure, I had seen many advertised products fail, but I had seen others succeed, some fantastically so. What did the success stories have in common, I wondered? I scrutinized them, looking for the subtle differences that distinguished the winners from the losers, and four principles emerged. Those principles define an approach I call PyroMarketing.

PyroMarketing is a "new'" way to think about marketing—an effective method to deliver relevant messages to the right people and to foster their spread throughout society. Rather than trying to break through the cacophony with bolder, louder, and more intrusive tactics, PyroMarketing provides a repeatable approach that recognizes and accommodates individual differences, acknowledges the power of experience, and leverages the influence of passionate customers.

A handful of business books have hinted at various elements of this new approach and some successful advertising campaigns have, perhaps unknowingly, followed a few of its tenets. This book, however, brings it all together. It organizes its principles into a four-step approach you, and everyone in your organization, can easily learn and apply.

My background is in Christian publishing and so this book will sometimes use examples and illustrations from that industry as I explain PyroMarketing. I will write often about *The Passion of the Christ* or a book called *The Purpose-Driven® Life,* or even about the life and ministry of Jesus, as I demonstrate PyroMarketing's power. But—and this is important—these principles are *not* limited to books or Christian products. With very few exceptions, they will work for you too.

In an article titled "How to Read a Business Book," *Fast Company* magazine correctly noted recently that "business books are necessarily about generalizations; your company is necessarily all about specifics. No one strategy or approach to marketing, no matter how brilliant, can be an exact fit."[1] That is true for PyroMarketing as well. As you read this book, don't try to apply each example exactly. Instead, first understand the PyroMarketing principle before asking yourself how it applies to your business. I've tried to explain, and provide evidence for, PyroMarketing's basic principles. With a few exceptions, I've left their application up to you because you know your business better than anyone else.

That same *Fast Company* article went on to suggest that readers distill all business books down to the handful of ideas that represent their core message. This is good advice since it is easy to lose sight of the big picture as you read your way through an entire book. If you lose your way while reading *PyroMarketing*, you can return to the introduction and regain your bearings. The next paragraph distills the essence of this entire book.

The societal influences that allowed mass marketing to prosper have disappeared, rendering mass marketing ineffective. New circumstances have created an opportunity for a different marketing approach, called PyroMarketing. It involves four steps.

1. Promote to the people most likely to buy.
2. Give them an experience with your product or service.
3. Help them tell others.
4. Keep a record of who they are.

This book captures this process and how it can be successfully applied to any product or service. It is as easy to learn as building a campfire and its principles are revealed in the lines of a song you may have sung while sitting beside one.

It only takes a spark to get fire going
And soon all those around can warm up in its glowing;
That's how it is with God's love,
Once you've experienced it,
You spread the love to everyone
You want to pass it on.

There are four steps to creating successful marketing campaigns. You build them the same way you build a campfire. If you were a scout or a camper, you already know the drill.

GATHER THE DRIEST TINDER

It only takes a spark to get a fire going.

You can start a fire with a single spark, but only if you begin with the material *most likely* to light. You start a successful marketing campaign the same way, with the people most likely to buy. They are the driest tinder. The driest tinder are so inclined toward your product or service that the slightest application of heat from your marketing moves them past their ignition temperature and sets them alight.

Relevance is the key. Relevance, more than reach, more than frequency, more than creativity, more than anything else, determines whether your message will sell your product or alienate the consumer. Your product or service and its marketing message are most relevant to the driest tinder.

Who are the driest tinder for your product or service? What makes them so interested? What makes them so valuable? We will explore the driest tinder in Chapter 3.

TOUCH IT WITH THE MATCH

Once you've experienced it.

Touching it with the match means, to the extent you can, giving people an experience with your product or service. If you want them to laugh, don't tell them you're funny; tell them a joke. There is no faster way to move people to purchase than by letting them actually experience the benefits you claim.

There are many ways to help people experience the benefits of your product or service and you'll be amazed by the power in this approach. Touching it with the match is the subject of Chapter 4.

FAN THE FLAMES

You spread the love to everyone. You want to pass it on.

After touching the driest tinder with the match, you've made the sale, but that's not where the process ends. The secret to a successful marketing campaign, like the key to building a campfire, isn't adding matches, it's fanning the flames. Fanning the flames means equipping people to spread your message through word of mouth. If they bought and love your product or service, they are ready to exponentially expand the reach of your marketing by telling others. Once you understand why this is true, you can enhance the process with tactics and tools that help your customers spread the word to their network of like-minded friends. Properly equipped they can convince people whose purchase threshold was far beyond the reach of your marketing.

SAVE THE COALS

Keep a record of those who care.

Traditional marketers spend budget after budget trying to find the same buyers—building the same fire—over and over again. They lure consumers from the masses with their promotions, but let them slip anonymously back into the crowd after they buy. You can't contact them if you don't know who they are. Naturally, if you can't contact them, you can't encourage word of mouth or promote future products either. Traditional mass marketing is like renting an apartment where new money is required for each month you stay. Traditional marketers spend each new budget to find many of the same people who bought the last time.

PyroMarketers save the coals. Saving the coals means keeping a record of the people who respond to your marketing so you can contact them, quickly and affordably, the next time you have something of interest, or mobilize them to promote your business to their family and friends. PyroMarketing is more like buying a house. Marketing becomes an investment. Each new campaign is a payment building equity for the future. Before long you own a segment of the market outright and can use new marketing resources to build new fires.

PyroMarketing is simple and it really works. Some recent examples provide impressive proof.

The Passion of the Christ, a movie depicting the suffering, death, and resurrection of Jesus, became a box office smash, grossing over $551 million worldwide in its first nine weeks despite the use of obscure foreign languages, an R rating, English subtitles, the lack of a major distributor, and a comparatively modest marketing budget. Yet, it is the highest-grossing R-rated movie of all time and the most successful independent film ever. Following its theatrical re-release for Easter 2005, it may well be the highest-grossing film of all time.

The Purpose-Driven® Life, a book explaining God's five purposes for successful living, authored by a Southern Baptist minister known primarily in religious circles, sold nearly one million copies each month from its release in October of 2002 through the summer of 2004 and continues at a best-selling pace. It sold more copies than any other book in America for 2003 and again in 2004, beating titles by the biggest names in publishing and outselling the next-best-selling nonfiction title by a factor of ten! *Publisher's Weekly* called it the best-selling hardcover book in American history.

Christianity, founded by an itinerant Jewish carpenter before the advent of telephones, television, instant messaging, press kits, the Internet, motorized transportation, or even the printing press, has prospered for over two thousand years, growing to become the world's largest religion with two billion adherents, some of whom have sacrificed their lives for the faith.

How do such phenomena occur? How does their popularity rise so quickly, spread so far, and endure so long? Why are people so passionate about them, giving their money, their time—even their lives—in support? And how can businesspeople foster similar zeal toward their products, service, or cause?

The success of *The Purpose-Driven® Life*, *The Passion of the Christ*, or of Christianity, remains puzzling to many, but not to those who know their secret. Whethter ministering the gospel or marketing a movie, they each followed a simple, four-step communication process I call PyroMarketing, and so can you.

BARRIERS BURNED AWAY

It began around nine o'clock on Sunday evening October 8, 1871, somewhere in the vicinity of the O'Leary barn. Apart from these few facts, little is known about the exact origin of the Great Chicago Fire. Though competing legends persist, the most common is that a cow belonging to Mrs. Catherine O'Leary kicked over a lantern, igniting the contents of a barn laden with a winter's provision of coal, wood shavings, and hay. Though mystery surrounds its beginning, the fire's subsequent growth is well documented.

It had been an especially dry autumn as, in the words of nineteenth-century historian A. T. Andreas, "nature had withheld her accustomed measure of prevention, and man had added to the peril by recklessness."[2] The city's dry wooden buildings, constructed one next to the other, offered little resistance to the advancing flames. Driven by strong winds from the southwest, the fire raced across them like a fuse, burning an unpredictable path toward the city's center. By 1:30 AM it reached the courthouse. Ninety minutes later it had consumed the Palmer House and the offices of the *Chicago Tribune*, pursuing thousands of residents as they evacuated to the safety of the city's North Division. By Monday noon the fire had reached the city's northern limit. It took a saving rain on Tuesday morning to finally blunt its progress and quench its insatiable flame. At last, exhausted Chicagoans had a reprieve from their retreat and a moment to look back, over their shoulders, at the smoldering ruins of their city.

Every end is a beginning. To characterize the Great Chicago Fire only as a tragedy misses its greater impact. While it destroyed one Chicago, it gave birth to another. In 1871, 300,000 residents mourned all they had lost to the fire, but today 8 million Chicagoans can celebrate the vigorous future it helped them find.[3] "The world as it is to people of this vicinity, has changed," one resident wrote days after the disaster, "an age has closed, and a new epoch . . . is about to begin."[4] Fire transformed the people of Chicago by showing them a surprising new opportunity.

On Wednesday, October 11, 1871, the *Chicago Tribune* published a half sheet of paper with a story about the fire and an editorial that began: "CHEER UP. In the midst of a calamity without parallel in the world's history, looking upon the ashes of thirty years' accumulation, the people of this once beautiful city have resolved that CHICAGO SHALL RISE AGAIN!" And rise it did.

Within seven years the city's population had nearly doubled.

A decade later it eclipsed one million, fulfilling the prophecy of wealthy Chicago booster John Stephen Wright, who predicted, "Five years will give Chicago more men, more money, more business, than she would have had without this fire."

Construction on more than eight miles of street frontage began within one year of the fire. Buildings of brick, stone, and iron replaced the shoddy wood plank construction that marked prefire Chicago. In 1885 the city became home to the first skyscraper by erecting the Home Insurance Building to a height of nine stories. Rather than load-bearing walls, it used a skeletal frame to support the building's weight: a novel design that took construction to unprecedented heights. The people of the city were not merely rebuilding what they had lost; they were building something entirely new and markedly better.

Among the art and literature inspired by the fire was a novel written by a minister, Edward Payson Roe, titled *Barriers Burned Away*. In the love story, Dennis Fleet tries to win the affection of Christine Ludolph, the daughter of a wealthy art dealer, but her atheism and aristocratic arrogance stand in the way. During the fire, however, Christine loses her wealth, her father, and her unbelief, declaring, "All barriers are burned away;" she embraces God, Dennis, and a new life.

The accumulations of our past can exert a terrible influence on our possible futures. Their weight, hanging around our necks like an albatross, can limit our choice of path and pace. The Great Chicago Fire destroyed large sections of the city, but it was also a purifying event that burned away the barriers to a dynamic new future. Unencumbered by the past, the people of Chicago were free to chart a new and fantastically successful course. A similar opportunity awaits you.

Set aside what you know about marketing; it may be a

barrier to a new and better future. Like the people of Chicago, you might discover that the accumulations of the last thirty years are only slowing you down. Leave them behind, turn the page, and let the fire begin.

From Floods to Flames

Every creative act involves . . . a new innocence of perception,
liberated from the cataract of accepted belief.
—Arthur Koestler, *The Sleepwalkers*, 1959

BLAST FROM THE PAST

The movie *Blast from the Past* opens in Los Angeles, where, in
1962, amid the heightening tensions of the Cuban missile cri-
sis an eccentric inventor named Calvin whisks his pregnant
wife to the safety of the bomb shelter he built beneath their
backyard. At the same moment a military training jet is experiencing engine trouble high overhead. Its pilot ejects just
before the plane careens into part of the family's home, triggering a series of fantastic explosions. Mistaking the crash for
a nuclear strike, Calvin and his wife Helen lock the doors to
the shelter and hunker down to wait out the radiation's thirty-
five-year half-life.

Not long afterward Helen goes into labor and, believing
their son is the first child born in a postapocalyptic world,
they name him Adam. For the next three and a half decades,
the family lives in the shelter, waiting for the radiation to sub-

side. Underground they eat, sleep, and entertain themselves by watching episodes of *The Honeymooners* on 8-millimeter film and educate Adam as he grows. Though many years pass, for the family in the shelter, time stands still.

One morning in 1997 the family awakens to an alarm signaling the day of their liberation. The time has come to venture outside. Equipped with a collection of baseball cards, a shopping list, and $3,000 in cash, Adam sets out on a mission to replenish the family's depleted supplies while his parents wait in the shelter. A hilarious sequence of misadventures follows as he encounters and promptly alienates various residents of modern-day Los Angeles. Through it all Adam remains blissfully unaware, never realizing that his innocent advances and naive attempts to socialize are driving away the very people he longs to meet. He has spent the last thirty-five years learning and perfecting the skills he will need to survive in this new world only to discover that they no longer work and, worse, that he knows no other way. The world has not waited for him. Things have changed and the techniques from 1962 his parents have taught him—tactics that worked so brilliantly thirty-five years before and seemed perfectly sensible in the safety of the shelter—completely fail him in the real, modern world.

Near the beginning of the film, before hiding in the shelter, Calvin is talking with a friend at a cocktail party. "There currently exists a type of neon light that lasts for five years," he says. "But you won't see it on the market. Same is true of batteries. I could take your simple yacht battery and rig it to last a decade, easily." "Well," his friend asks rhetorically, "what the heck kind of marketing system can't get great new products like that out to the public?"[1] Sadly, it's the marketing system you and your business are probably still using.

THE END OF AN ERA

The era of mass marketing is ending. The promotion of a single product or service to everyone through undifferentiated media reached its peak in the 1960s and its success convinced most marketers it was the only way. But the world has changed and mass tactics that worked so brilliantly thirty-five years before and which still seem perfectly sensible in the safety of the boardroom increasingly fail in the real, modern world. But don't take my word for it. Plenty of others are sounding the alarm. Larry Light, McDonald's chief marketing officer, recently declared that mass marketing no longer works.[2] Trend prophet Faith Popcorn predicts, "The scatter-shot advertising approach, which wasn't necessarily all that effective in the past, will be even less so in the 21st century."[3] And, in a special report titled "The Vanishing Mass Market," *BusinessWeek* cautioned that new technology, product proliferation, and fragmented media were creating a whole new world—a world in which mass marketing could not compete. Smart companies, according to *BusinessWeek*, are "standing mass marketing on its head by shifting emphasis from selling to the vast, anonymous crowd to selling to millions of particular consumers."[4] Yet many companies continue to use mass marketing, hoping it still wields its old influence.

But, if old definitions of marketing were still true, then eToys should be a thriving business. Founded in 1997, this Internet toy retailer spent 60 percent of its revenue on what it thought was effective advertising, including $20 million on an elaborate campaign during the Christmas shopping season. Such an aggressive promotional campaign should have ensured success, yet fifteen months later, eToys was bankrupt.[5]

Two-thirds of all the commercials in the Super Bowl of

2000 were for Internet companies. The Super Bowl is generally considered the year's best advertising opportunity, but this game was even more. It was one of the most-watched television programs of all time. The St. Louis Rams' stirring 23-16 victory over the Tennessee Titans was not secured until the game's final play. Unlike the blowouts of Super Bowls past, this game surged back and forth, keeping viewers riveted to their screens for the entire contest. The game garnered a whopping 43.2 Nielsen rating and an impressive 62 market share, a 7 percent increase from the previous year.[6] An estimated 130 million viewers[7] absorbed every play, along with advertising for Pets.com. Later that same year Pets.com couldn't find either a buyer or additional financing and disappeared without leaving so much as a stain on the carpeting.[8]

In a single year Art.com, AutoConnect.com, CarsDirect.com, Drugstore.com, Homestore.com, Living.com, Petstore.com, RealEstate.com, and Rx.com spent a combined $169 million on traditional advertising. How can it be that most people have never heard of them?[9]

IN THE BEGINNING

Mass marketing didn't always disappoint. There was a time when it dominated and the memory of that dominance is why so many marketers are reluctant to give it up. What they must remember is that marketing systems don't exist in isolation. They are one component in a stew of societal influences and their efficacy depends on that context. It's similar to the situation faced by every boat. A ship floats because its hull is shaped to displace water, but only if there is water to displace. Remove the water and you will ground the ship. The circumstances surrounding the development of mass marketing were as important as the marketing system they empowered. By itself mass marketing possessed no special powers. It worked because a confluence of societal currents swelled a storm surge that lifted mass marketing throughout most of the twentieth century.

Many experts trace mass marketing's headwaters to the start of the industrial revolution. Frederick W. Taylor's book *The Principles of Scientific Management* encouraged businesses to trade craftsmanship for production efficiencies and revolutionized manufacturing just as the assembly line, division of labor, and affordable clocks and watches made those efficiencies both possible and measurable. The electric light erased the distinction between day and night so that products people used only when they were awake were now also being made as they slept. With these improvements came economies of scale. The declining cost curve was born and, for the first time, the more products a business made, the cheaper each unit became. Since the factory and labor costs were fixed, companies maximized their profits by increasing production. The industrial revolution created a plentiful supply of new, identical products and, as warehouses swelled with the surplus, an acute need for an effective way to sell them.

Retailing was undergoing a revolution as well. Between the Civil War and the beginning of the new century the department store appeared. Called "palaces of consumption" by historian Daniel Boorstin, they were a single, large retail shop located in the central city that sold everything to everyone.[10] In addition to replacing a downtown's-worth of specialty boutiques with a single place to buy, they wrought another, unexpected change—a single price to pay. No longer would Americans negotiate every purchase, because prices, like the products to which they were attached, were standardized. Department stores sold commodity items at fixed prices to undifferentiated people, which contributed to what Boorstin called "the leveling of America." The distinctive boutiques that once had met people's specialized needs with custom products at negotiable prices were disappearing faster than department store inventories.

Consumer demand was also increasing and, with the exception of the Great Depression, grew steadily through the first half of the twentieth century. People no longer used or rented things; they owned them instead. In *The Americans*, Boorstin writes: "Ownership was enjoyed by unprecedented numbers. What they owned was not only land and houses and cattle and the tools of their trade, the traditional 'property' of recorded history. This new nation produced new kinds of property. The automobile was only one of innumerable objects that were manufactured in such large numbers and so widely desired that their ownership came to seem a standard of subsistence."[11] World War II influenced consumer demand even further. As men sailed overseas to fight, women took their place in the factories. Though America was at full employment, it was difficult to spend because the government had rationed so many consumer goods. Only war bonds were in ample supply and as families invested in them, their accumulated wealth grew. The dam broke when the war ended, unleashing a torrent of well-financed consumer demand. In addition to that, the postwar boom of babies produced a bumper crop of new consumers that has influenced the economy ever since. At last, consumer demand matched manufacturing's new and improved ability to supply.

To this point American society had consisted of isolated regional communities, but its transformation into a single national mass culture was helped along by the emergence of national mass media, an innovation that began with magazines. In 1790, the country's print media consisted of ninety-two newspapers and just seven magazines with tiny reader-ships in highly localized settings.[12] But by 1900, broadly popular magazines like *Munsey's, McClures, The Ladies Home Journal,* and *Cosmopolitan* were serving audiences in the hundreds of thousands.[13]   Suddenly citizens of Philadelphia were discussing the same news or entertainment stories as readers in San Francisco. America was leveling some more.

Soon the country was awash in broadcasting too. Commercial radio was born in 1920 when KDKA in Pittsburgh aired the first commercial broadcast.[14] By 1950 two thousand commercial stations broadcast their signals to more than 75 million radios, a number that increased until, by 1960, the average American household had 3 radios and there were 40 million more in its cars![15]

Television, a brand-new way to "mass produce the moment," joined radio a short time later.[16] By 1931 there were 40,000 television sets in America—9,000 in New York City alone. In 1950 barely 10 percent of American homes had televisions, but by 1959—just nine years later—the figure had swollen to 90 percent. The medium delivered audiences of unprecedented size. Three networks supplied all the programming and, from comedies to commercials, Americans soaked it up. By airing a spot simultaneously on ABC, NBC, and CBS, an advertiser in the 1960s could reach 80 percent of American women.[17] While television unified the masses, it also fostered a new segregation by dividing America between the people who made television programming (the ruling class) and those who consumed it (the proletariat) replacing the give and take of conversation with a "one-way window."[18] The mass media age was born.

With mass media came mass advertising. Ad spending increased spectacularly, rising from $50 million in 1867 to $22.4 billion in 1974.[19] Whereas salesmen once persuaded individual consumers, advertising now sought to persuade large groups. As it relentlessly tried to widen the audience and broaden a product's appeal, it further democratized an increasingly homogeneous America.

At the same time the population was shifting. In 1870 the US Census first officially distinguished the urban from the rural. In 1910 the nation experienced another first as more Americans lived in and around its cities than in rural areas. Suburbs grew as highways and mass transportation linked city centers with their surroundings.[20] People who previously had rented urban apartments bought their own homes and found they faced an entirely new quandary. For the first time in their lives they had a front yard but not the slightest notion of what to do with it. In the *St. James Encyclopedia of Popular Culture*, Richard Digby-Junger writes: "Owners struggled to define what was appropriate and necessary for the proper exterior images of their homes. Individuality was prized, but exhibitionism was not, and a degree of uniformity came to be considered a virtue."[21] Not only did homes look alike, so did the neighborhoods and cities in which they were built.

"The uniqueness of America," wrote Daniel Boorstin, "would prove to be its ability to erase uniqueness."[22] Anyplace became more like everyplace. People lived in the same cities, they consumed the same media, and they even decorated their front yards alike. Homogeneous masses were pooling near America's cities; the gathering headwaters of an imminent mass marketing flood.

Somewhere toward the middle of the twentieth century, the tributaries of mass manufacturing—high demand for consumer products, a predominantly urban population, and a few but pervasive mass media—converged. The formula for mass marketing's success was this:

Limited Product Choice but Plentiful Supplies

+

High Demand for Goods and Services

+

Clustered Consumers

+

Broad Access to Very Few Media

+

Little or No Consumer Resistance to Advertising

=

Mass Marketing Works Very Well

It was, in the lyrics of Donald Fagan, "a glorious time to be free." It was an even more glorious time to be a mass marketer. They called all the shots. They decided what products to make, what colors they came in, where they would be promoted and sold. Mass marketing worked because conformity was a virtue. The audience was large and homogeneous, transforming America into "generica."[23] Vast monolithic blocks of eyeballs were fixed on just three television channels, eagerly awaiting every advertisement. Media were centrally controlled and an elite few set their agenda. With a small number of spots mass marketers could introduce their new gizmo to an entire nation. Stores carried the same brands and people saw all the same advertisements. Mass marketing ruled the society it helped create.

LEAVING THE SHELTER

In 1903 man's feet left the earth as Orville Wright made the first successful flight in a powered aircraft. Just sixty-six years later they stepped onto the moon when Neil Armstrong low-

ered himself from the Apollo 11 lunar module. What a difference a few years makes.

Charles Francis Adams Jr. understood this when, as the first
transcontinental railroad was nearing completion in 1868, he
forecast both the innovation's power to transform the American
experience and people's futile resistance to that change. "Perhaps
if the existing community would take now and then the trouble
to pass in review the changes it has already witnessed it would be
less astounded at the revolutions which continually do and continually must flash before it; perhaps also it might with more
grace accept the inevitable, and cease from the useless attempts
at making a wholly new world conform itself to the rules and theories of a bygone civilization."[24]

Open the door to the shelter, then, and "take now the trouble to pass in review the changes" we have witnessed since
mass marketing's zenith. Cultural shifts and technological
innovations as influential as those that created mass marketing have conspired to siphon away its dominance. Consumer
demand remains, but we now live in a world of expansive
product choice, dispersed populations, myriad media outlets,
and consumer resistance to advertising so strong it borders
on resentment. The environmental factors that once lifted
mass marketing's ship no longer exist and it has run aground.

HAVE IT YOUR WAY

Countless product choices now allow consumers to express
their individuality with every purchase. Mass production has
given way to mass customization; the evidence for this
abounds. The number of brands on supermarket shelves has
tripled since 1993. In 2003 alone some 26,893 new food and
household products were introduced, according to Mintel

International Group Ltd.'s Global New Products Database.[25] Among them were 115 new deodorants, 187 breakfast cereals, and 303 women's perfumes. At the height of mass marketing a single telephone utility served the entire nation. Today you can choose from a bevy of local, long-distance, and cellular providers. To see a movie in the early 1970s you had to go to the theater; today you can watch it on cable, order pay-per-view via satellite, or rent a VHS cassette or DVD. You can watch it at home, from your laptop computer at a coffee shop, or from the backseat of your car on the interstate.

Consumers have choices as never before and those choices feature subtle distinctions that improve their appeal to narrowly defined audience niches. Masses of products with individual appeal have replaced products with mass appeal.

DISPERSED POPULATIONS

Urban planner Witold Rybczynski observed that the American population is decentralizing faster than any other society in history. Populations that once huddled around cities like boy scouts around a campfire have left, choosing instead to scatter along the highways that connect them. People in established suburbs are leaving, pressing farther beyond into what *New York Times* columnist David Brooks calls "exurbs." According to Brooks: "Ninety percent of the office space built in America in the 1990's was built in suburbia, usually in low office parks along the interstates," he writes. "Now you have a tribe of people who not only don't work in cities, they don't commute to cities or go to the movies in cities, or have any contact with urban life. You have these huge sprawling communities with no center."[26] Homogeneous masses are no longer pooling in America's cities. They are, instead, sprinkled across her landscape in a trend exactly opposite the migration that empowered mass marketing. In 1970, Los Angeles spread its population of seven million across 450 square miles and had no dominant downtown. It "offered the visual future of American cities in caricature."[26]

More damaging than the physical sprawl, is the attitude behind it. Suburbs and cities are estranged because suburbs, in the words of Rybczynski, "have withdrawn into a cocoon of smug autonomy." But a decentralized society exhibiting smug autonomy cannot support the lock-step attitudes and common opinions mass marketing requires. Mass marketing thrived when dependent consumers were bound to cities and their centrally controlled mass media, but wilts in a world of evenly dispersed independent thinkers.

FRAGMENTED MEDIA

"Too many establishments' communications programs run on the suppositions of mass communications, specifically, that the mass audience is like a herd of sheep that can be led to commercial and political slaughter," wrote William Gargan, predicting the demise of traditional advertising in the pages of *Triangle Business Journal* more than a dozen years ago. "People will not believe words out of sync with undeniable reality."[28]

It is impossible to treat the masses like sheep as marketers once did, because mass audiences no longer exist. And if they did exist, you couldn't herd them as before because a tiny clutch of centrally controlled mass media has splintered into a dizzying array of new choices whose consumption the individual controls. In 1820 there were just 25 daily papers in the United States. By 1999 there were 2,388 daily or Sunday papers representing the highest number of newspapers with the highest circulation for any country in the world.[29] By the same token, a handful of magazines existing in 1900 burgeoned to nearly 10,000 by 1999. And while these increases represent volatile growth for traditional media, they pale in comparison with the explosion of information made possible by the World Wide Web.

In 2001, Google reported a new record; for the first time the Internet's most popular search engine gave its users access to over one billion Web pages—one page for every sixth person on the planet. What Google didn't mention when announcing its accomplishment was that the Web is growing even faster.[30] Similar fragmentation, albeit on a smaller scale, is afflicting television.

The television remote control ended institutional dominance and control of mass media by stripping power from network boardrooms and placing it under the consumer's thumb. The consumer has always had the power to tune in or out, but was reluctant to exercise it in decades past because tuning out meant being uninformed. But "narrowcasting," which began with the advent of cable television in the 1970s and continues via satellite, has simultaneously narrowed the focus of program content while multiplying its availability. Five hundred channels of special interest programming have replaced three general networks and the proliferation of media means that today people don't have to turn the television off; they can simply change the channel. Instead of choosing between feast and famine, consumers select a particular informational diet from a buffet of options.

Mass media no longer exist because there are now nearly as many media choices as people to consume them. Though all media have fragmented, it's easiest to see the effect by watching television. The medium that once illustrated mass marketing's success now forecasts its demise.

FRAGMENTATION NATION

There was a time, just a few decades ago, when you could watch Lucille Ball in *I Love Lucy* or watch *The Honeymooners* or *The Ed Sullivan Show,* and know that you were sharing the experience with nearly every other American. Television had become the great societal unifier.[31] It was easy to discuss your favorite show with friends the next day at work because you could be assured nearly everyone had watched the same program. But as television's popularity increased, so did the number of programming choices, with a devastating impact on the medium's power.

According to Nielsen Media Research, the number of channels received by the average American household soared from nineteen in 1985 to forty-nine in 1997, to more than one hundred today! The fragmentation of television parallels the fragmentation of personal interest and the loss of shared experience. In his book *Bowling Alone,* Harvard researcher Robert D. Putnam notes the significance of this trend:

> The ability of television to create a single national "water-cooler" has shrunk, as fewer and fewer of us watch common programs. In the early 1950's two-thirds of all Americans tuned in and watched the top-rated programs (*I Love Lucy*); in the early 1970's the top-rated program (*All in the Family*) drew about half of the national TV audience; by the mid 1990s the audience share of *ER* and *Seinfeld* was barely one-third. This trend toward market segmentation provides choice and presumably thus enhances consumer satisfaction, but it also undercuts TV's once vaunted role in bringing us together.[32]

Television programs are no longer experiences we share with large groups of other people. Consequently, people have less in common. We have become a nation of strangers. I have personally never seen an episode of *Survivor*. I couldn't debate with you whether a participant's dismissal from the island was long overdue or a miscarriage of justice. I have never watched an entire episode of *Who Wants to Be a Millionaire?*, though the program did unify Americans in their disdain for the catchphrase it wrought. And yes, that is my final answer.

Common experience and centralized control have given way to individual control of unique media experiences.

Common experience and the belief that we are similar to the people around us, as we will see in Chapter 5, "Fan the Flames," was essential to the incredible popularity of *The Purpose-Driven®️ Life* and *The Passion of the Christ* and it is just as vital to the campaigns for your product or service. Yet the fragmentation of formerly mass media makes it nearly impossible to achieve common experience through them as you once could.

FEWER VIEWERS WATCHING LESS

It wasn't that long ago that three major networks, ABC, CBS, and NBC, claimed the majority of the television viewing audience. As recently as 1980 they enjoyed a commanding 90 percent share. By 1983 that share had fallen to 74 percent, a smaller but still dominant percentage. By 2002–3, however, viewership of traditional broadcast networks had plunged to just 38.4 percent, despite the addition of several new networks including Fox, UPN, WB, and PAX. In fact, with the exception of a 1-point increase in 1993–94, network television viewership has been caught in a downward spiral for almost thirty years— losing 41.5 percent since 1977[33]—with no end in sight.[34]

DROWNING IN ADS

You'd think that with the fragmentation of the viewing audience, the overall decline in viewers, and a reduction in the time spent watching, that television advertising would be on the decline as well. Not so.

A television broadcast hour is divided between the show (programming) and advertisements (nonprogramming), either for products or other television shows. Daytime nonprogramming time in the United States has risen, astonishingly, to almost 21 minutes per hour. More than a third of every television hour then is devoted to advertising and promotion. Even in Canada, where the government regulates this percentage, nonprogramming is on the increase—jumping to an all-time high of 16.4 minutes per hour despite a legal limit of 12.0. So much advertising clogs sports broadcasts that TiVo owners can begin watching a digitally recorded football game just as the live event enters the third quarter and, by skipping the commercials, catch up to the live broadcast by the two-minute warning so they can watch the game's final moments as they occur. No wonder people are watching less television programming; there is less television *programming* to watch.

TUNE IN AND TUNE OUT

Fewer Americans are watching television, but what of those who remain? What kind of consumers are television advertisers spending millions of dollars to reach anyway? The picture isn't very pretty.

Television has become antisocial. Not only has it segregated the manufacturer from the consumer, thereby making it harder to discern their wants and needs; it has isolated consumers from each other as well. The medium that once unified a nation now divides it. Research surveys have found that husbands and wives spend three to four times more time watching television than talking to each other and six to seven times more than they spend in activities outside the home. Increasingly, those Americans who still watch television do it alone. As the number of television sets per household increases, so does the incidence of solitary viewing. Husbands watch alone in the family room, while wives watch another program in the bedroom; even the children have their own set. One study suggests that at least half of all Americans watch entirely alone.[35]

Striking evidence for television-sponsored civic disengagement comes from a remarkable study conducted during the 1970s in three isolated northern Canadian towns before the advent of the VCR or satellite TV. For the study the towns were named Notel, Unitel, and Multitel. The communities, except for differing television reception, were typical and essentially the same. Notel, owing only to poor reception due to its location in a valley, received no television signal at the start of the study. Unitel, as its name suggests, received a single television channel, the Canadian Broadcasting Corporation (CBC). Residents of Multitel could receive four channels, the CBC and three American commercial networks.

During the course of the two-year study a single television channel (CBC) was introduced to Notel residents. Unitel reception was expanded to include the three American commercial networks. Multitel reception remained unchanged throughout the duration of the study.

The results clearly showed that the beginning of television for Notel residents meant the end of their involvement in social activities. Canadian researcher Tannis MacBeth Williams and her colleagues concluded: "Residents are more likely to be centrally involved in their community's activities in the absence than in the presence of television."[36]

Not only are heavy television viewers less likely to be active in community affairs, they're less likely to be active at all. Studies of television find that of all household activities, television requires the lowest level of concentration, alertness, challenge, and skill. People don't watch because they enjoy television. On the contrary, research shows, people prefer myriad leisure activities including cooking and housework to watching the tube. "TV's dominance in our lives," says Putnam, "reflects not its sublime pleasures, but its minimal costs." People watch TV out of laziness.

Television has become a surrogate for real interpersonal relationships by divorcing social ties from physical encounters. Americans sit alone in their homes—zombies, with blue light shifting on their faces—mentally stoking a false connection with the characters on the screen. Communications theorist Joshua Meyrowitz puts it this way: "Electronic media creates ties and associations that compete with those formed through live interaction in specific locations. Live encounters are certainly more 'special' and provide stronger and deeper relationships, but their relative number is decreasing."[37]

Americans occupy parallel realities, composed of the real lives they live and the televised world into which they sometimes escape. It is futile to buy one more meaningless advertising minute targeting the artificial part of people's lives. To be a PyroMarketer you must speak to real people, associating with real friends, living real lives, and able to really act upon your message.

There was a day when television spoke with one voice to the entire nation, drawing us together through shared experience. It was a single, but important element, in a well-rounded American lifestyle that included community involvement and social interaction. But now, television, like its mass media counterparts, is a badly fragmented medium most likely to reach lonely, disconnected, passive, depressed people, disinclined to leave their homes either to buy your product or to tell others about it. By promoting isolation and disengagement, television sows apathy and destroys social networks—the very networks instrumental to the success of *The Purpose-Driven® Life, The Passion of the Christ,* and to your product or service. Television advertising, once king of electronic mass media and the poster child for mass marketing, has lost its potency.

The watershed supplying mass marketing has evaporated. The tributaries of plentiful products but limited choice, clustered consumers, broad access to very few media, and little or no resistance to advertising are but dry riverbeds—reminders of a bygone era. The rainy season that lifted mass marketing's hull has passed, replaced by a dry season and its new realities.

Vast Product Choice and Plentiful Supplies

+

Dispersed Consumers

+

High Demand for Goods and Service

+

Broad Access to Myriad Media

+

High Consumer Resistance—Even Resentment—
Toward Advertising

=

Mass Marketing No Longer Works

DOING A NEW THING

Astonishingly, the only vestige of that bygone era is the marketing approach it spawned. Traditional mass marketing persists because mass media perpetuate it, but also because marketing people allow it to. You must resist the pressure to continue using traditional mass marketing. It's time to leave the past behind, forget what you learned in the shelter, and commit instead to doing a new thing—the right thing. It is not a subtle change. The differences between traditional mass marketing and PyroMarketing are striking and clear, and that's good, because you will know when you are on the right path.

Several dichotomies distinguish traditional mass marketing from PyroMarketing and are as different as the rainy season from the dry.

MASS MARKETING	PYROMARKETING
Homogeneity (people are the same)	Heterogeneity (people are different)
Focus on the company	Focus on the consumer
Cost per thousand	Cost per customer
Marketing Immerses	Marketing Ignites
Advertising puffery	Advertising honesty

Homogeneity

Mass marketing assumes that people are essentially the same. It's an easy mistake to make and one that follows, quite naturally, from mass manufacturing. Mass manufacturing, after all, was designed to make standardized, homogeneous products. Assembly lines optimized their sameness to exacting specifications.[38] It's a small, but errant, step to conclude that consumers are as interchangeable as the products they buy.

Through an error of logic, mass marketers attempt to use demographics to define whole populations. If the person who bought the book was rich, they conclude, rich people are book buyers and they should target them with their advertising. It may be that the person who bought the book was wealthy, but it doesn't follow that all or most wealthy people buy books. People are defined by many attributes and they don't all contribute to purchase decisions. If we asked the woman why she bought the book, she probably would not say, "Because I'm rich!" More likely she would say something like, "I bought the novel to read on vacation." Or, "A friend told me it was wonderful."

By focusing on characteristics irrelevant to the actual purchase decision, mass marketers can be duped into thinking people are alike.

Heterogeneity

PyroMarketers know people are different: Each one is a distinctive blend of characteristics, experiences, interests, and passions only some of which contribute to each purchase decision. Furthermore, those differences matter. Ignore them at your peril.

Say you manufactured caps embroidered with the logos of NFL football teams and were trying to find the best prospect for a Green Bay Packers hat. Would you target me, or my friend Ryan? You could study our demographics for clues, but you'd find little to distinguish one from the other. We are both about the same age and married with young children. We are both college educated and earning similar salaries. We live in the same community. We work for the same company. We are both football fans with the dish and NFL Sunday Ticket so we see every play when our favorite team competes. But you will sell a Green Bay Packers hat only to me. I will buy another even though I already own five or six because I love the Green Bay Packers. Ryan, on the other hand, will never buy because, despite a college education and other redeeming qualities that would seem to preclude such nonsense, he is a Vikings fan.

Mass Marketing Focuses on the Company

In about A.D. 150, the Egyptian astronomer Claudius Ptolemy put forth his view of the universe. He claimed the earth was a fixed, inert, immovable mass, located at the center of the universe, and all celestial bodies, including the sun and the stars, revolved around it. Like mass marketing, it was a theory that fit human nature. It seemed intuitively obvious to the casual observer, and it stroked man's ego.[39] It would be another 1,380 years before Copernicus would demonstrate that it was also completely wrong.

I attended a meeting recently, at a company I will not name, where new product ideas related to an author's new book were being discussed. The thinking focused on the company's goals. Each new product forced the consumer to buy some other product or service. The author's book drove people to a Web site. The Web site directed people to a seminar. The seminar was calculated to sell the book and other products during its breaks. The consumer was just a source of revenue and this company aimed to trap them in an endless cycle of purchases without ever actually helping them solve a problem or enjoy a benefit. When this became apparent, I raised my hand and asked, "What does the consumer want?" The company's president immediately replied, "Screw the consumer."

Traditional mass marketing imagines the universe revolving around the business. It operates from the inside out— beginning with the company's goals and often ignoring the consumer's entirely. It makes telemarketing calls at mealtime, sends spam e-mail, or disguises direct mail as urgent correspondence from a bank or the government. Mass marketing installs sidewalks at right angles and tells the consumer to stay off the grass.

PyroMarketing Focuses on the Consumer

"It's not about you." That's the first sentence of *The Purpose-Driven® Life,* but it is also the first rule of PyroMarketing. Stop thinking about your company and start thinking about your customers. PyroMarketing places the customer's needs first. It allows people to walk where they will and builds the sidewalks on the footpaths they wear.

Putting the customer first may seem counterintuitive, but it is, in fact, the best way to achieve your company's goals. Zig Ziglar, the legendary motivational speaker, business consultant, and student of human behavior, has preached for years that you can have anything in life you want if you just help enough other people get what they want. This is as true in marketing as it is in life.

When a religious leader asked Jesus which of the Ten Commandments was the most important, he replied that the most important was to love God with all your heart, soul, mind, and strength and that the second was to love your neighbor as yourself. He knew that if people obeyed only those two, they would never violate the others.

The greatest commandment for PyroMarketing is to love your customer as yourself. Don't try to sell them; try to serve them. If you serve them with your products, if you respect them with your marketing approach, if you put them first, then everything else will fall into place. You will meet your sales quotas, you will gain market share, and you will create an army of devoted customer evangelists with lifelong allegiance.

Mass Marketing Cares About Cost per Thousand

Cost per thousand, or CPM (M for Roman 1,000), measures the cost of reaching a thousand people with an ad. It is supposed to help businesses weigh the relative value of various advertising options. The vehicle with the lowest CPM is thought to be superior because it reaches the greatest number of people for the money. If mass marketing's other assumptions were true—if everyone is the same, if all people are equally likely to buy, if marketing can, in fact, coerce—then this makes perfect sense. If the essence of great marketing is nothing more than throwing advertising against the wall to see what sticks, then CPM matters a lot. The lower the CPM, the more you can throw.

However, this betrays one of mass marketing's fundamental flaws. Increasingly, it confuses activity with results. What does it matter how much you throw if none of it sticks? And by "sticking" I don't mean awareness or retention or mind share. It's not enough to place the ads, or to have them seen by lots of people. What happened as a result? Did anyone buy the advertised product?

PyroMarketing Cares About Cost per Customer

Cost per customer (CPC) is a better way to evaluate the relative merits of advertising. CPC doesn't measure how much you throw against the wall, it measures what sticks. I don't care how many people see an ad, I want to know how many will respond. A focus on the prospects most likely to respond leads you away from mass media and toward tactics you may not have considered.

Mass Marketing Immerses

Traditional mass marketing believes it can convince the disinterested. By a process that is arrogant and ill conceived, it tries to commandeer the attention of indifferent people and, by immersing them in advertising, create a felt need where none had previously existed. But this grossly overestimates advertising's power to persuade and the consumer's willingness to be persuaded. In the face of declining effectiveness and desperate for the consumer's elusive attention, mass marketers are opening the advertising floodgates.

Hippolytus de Marsiliis, a sixteenth-century Italian lawyer, invented what is commonly called "Chinese water torture." Apparently, after observing how drops of water falling one by one on a stone gradually eroded away a hollow, he decided to give it a try on a human body. It's a fair bet that ol' Hippolytus might have also pulled the wings off a few flies in his day.

In *The History of Torture,* author Brian Innes describes the ordeal. "Victims were strapped down so that they could not move, and cold water was then dripped slowly on to a small area of the body. The forehead was found to be the most suitable point for this form of torture: prisoners could see each drop coming, and were gradually driven frantic."[40]

Traditional mass marketing inflicts a similar torture on its innocent victims. The consumer is held hostage as companies try to extract what they want. Mass marketing repeatedly accosts them with advertising—drip, drip, drip—believing that eventually the consumer will "cry uncle" and buy the advertised product.

I give two thumbs down to the advertising that some theaters have begun showing prior to movies. Full-motion video commercials with surround sound are sometimes run at the time the feature was scheduled to begin. The lights are dimmed and, rather than the film they have paid to see, people are subjected to advertisements utilizing the full visual and aural power of the theater.

Not surprisingly the mass media companies offering the ads extol the supposed virtue of reaching a "captive audience."[41] The Web site for the ScreenVision Cinema Network brags, "We have a captive audience watching your advertisement. No interruptions! The patrons sitting in the theaters are not going anywhere."

But is that good? And, just how does that "captive audience" feel about its captivity and advertisers' attempts to exploit it? One famous moviegoer, Roger Ebert, the film reviewer for the *Chicago Sun-Times*, panned the practice and spoke for millions when he said, "I cannot understand why advertisers would want to attract hostility toward their products by deliberately offending potential customers."[42]

Other people have expressed their disgust by assembling protest organizations or starting Web sites. Www.didntialready-payforthismovie.com lists companies that advertise before movies and encourages people to boycott their products. Www.shinybluegrasshopper.com lists contact information for theater chains that show commercials so individuals can more easily write them to complain. CaptiveAudience.org has one primary goal: to urge theater owners to discontinue showing invasive, TV-like commercials before the beginnings of movies.[43] One

woman even initiated a class-action lawsuit against Loews Cine-
plex Entertainment Group over the practice.

Consumers don't like to be coerced. They'll see through
your attempts and they will resent you for them. So why try?
What good is a captive audience for your advertising message
if the moment they are freed they boycott your products,
organize protest groups, launch critical Web sites, or file
class-action lawsuits against your company? Trespassing on
the attention of the disinterested is counterproductive. You
want customer evangelists, not protest activists.

PyroMarketing Ignites

Marketing at its very best is communication, not coercion.
When you connect people to the products or services that sat-
isfy their needs, nothing more is required. When your product
and its marketing are relevant, people ignite and immersing
them isn't necessary. Immersive advertising proves the adage
that you can lead a horse to water but you cannot make it
drink, but PyroMarketing proves its corollary, that you cannot
prevent a thirsty horse from drinking.

Mass Marketing Allows Puffery

I bristle whenever I hear people say, "Oh, that's just marketing," because what they mean is, "Oh, that's just someone trying to trick me." Or, "Those claims are lies." How did marketing become synonymous with dishonesty? Why do people
equate advertising with deception? Traditional mass marketers have themselves to blame.

Technically, advertisers are not permitted to mislead people. Fraud is illegal. Practically, however, things are not so

plain. Courts have established that advertisers can make claims about their products or services that are "not meant to be taken literally." It's called puffery and it is permitted by the Uniform Commercial Code, a compendium of laws adopted by every state except Louisiana. It allows exaggerations because it assumes that reasonable people are smart enough to see through them. The UCC distinguishes between objective claims and puffery. Objective claims are specific, measurable, or based on fact. Puffery is more apt to be vague, immeasurable, or opinionated.

Recently a proposed change to the code was defeated. Had it passed, it would have shifted the burden of proof during advertising-related litigation. It would have required advertisers to prove their claims were puffery rather than making consumers prove they weren't. It provided that promotional claims constitute an agreement with buyers and would have held advertisers liable for their exaggerated claims. The advertising world threw a fit. Leading advertising associations formed a coalition and hired a law firm to fight the proposed change. Industry leaders have cried foul in articles. Lobbyists lobbied.

Puffery, they argued, is a benign means advertisers use to grab a consumer's attention. They are merely enlivening their ads with harmless hyperbole. What damage can it do? Puffery's exaggerations are obviously absurd.[44] No one out of diapers would take them literally. So, there is no need to limit advertisers to "dry factual statements."

However, exaggerating means "to enlarge beyond the bounds of truth" and hyperbole is "an extravagant exaggeration." In effect, some advertisers were pleading for permission to lie: to tell big, extravagant lies. They saw it as the only way to get the consumer's attention.

But if the claims of advertising puffery are obviously

absurd, why make them? Why fight for a consumer's attention only to squander it telling them apparent lies? That doesn't sell your product, or build your brand, or recruit customer evangelists, it merely convinces consumers you are dishonest, something many already suspected.

PyroMarketing Demands Advertising Honesty

PyroMarketers tell the truth. They don't need to lie. Factual statements are not dry when they honestly describe a benefit to the person who needs it most. Honesty fosters trust, the very opposite of their response to puffery and spin.

"Spin sets into motion a never-ending cycle of skepticism," wrote Malcolm Gladwell in a *New Yorker* article titled "The Spin Myth." "The curious thing about our contemporary obsession with spin, however, is that we seldom consider whether spin works. We simply assume that, because people everywhere are trying to manipulate us, we're being manipulated. Yet it makes just as much sense to assume the opposite: that the reason spin is everywhere today is that it doesn't work—that, because the public is getting increasingly inured to spin, spinners feel they must spin even harder, on and on, in an ever-escalating arms race." People are skeptical and, as Gladwell points out, "How we respond to a media proposition has at least as much to do with its pragmatic meaning (why we think the statement is being made) as with its semantic meaning (what is literally being said)."[45]

If you want people's attention, be attentive to their needs. If you want them to trust you, then be trustworthy. If you want them to believe you, tell them the truth. The golden rule of PyroMarketing is: Market to the consumer as you would have them market unto you.

ADAM AND EVE

In the movie *Blast from the Past,* discussed at the start of this chapter, Adam meets a girl named Eve who helps him understand the changes the world has undergone during the thirty-five years he and his family were sequestered in the shelter. Toward the end of the film they discover stock certificates in a cigar box with Adam's baseball cards—ten thousand shares of IBM, AT&T, and Polaroid dating from 1958 and worth millions of dollars. They buy some property and begin building a home where they can live with Adam's parents. Returning to share the good news, they catch Adam's folks climbing back into the shelter. Thinking the world has gone crazy, his dad plans to hide there for ten more years until "things return to normal." But Adam and Eve intervene.

"Our idea was to bring Adam's parents up to the surface very slowly," Eve says in a voice-over as we watch Adam and his father play catch with a baseball. "Make them very comfortable and then break the bad news to them that there was no nuclear holocaust. And if that doesn't kill them Adam's going to tell his father about the Internet."

You cannot return to the shelter either. Things will not return to "normal." The advice that Charles Francis Adams, Jr., gave in 1868 is still true today: "With grace you must accept the inevitable, and cease from useless attempts at making a wholly new world conform itself to the rules and theories of a bygone civilization."[46] I've tried to bring you up to the surface slowly and to break the news that the mass marketing era, what must have seemed like the Garden of Eden for American business, no longer exists. I'm assuming you already know about the Internet. And while you can never go back, you can move forward, but only if you learn a new way.

Today's business climate is far too dry to float mass marketing's boat, but drought conditions like these are just what you need to build a fire.

CHAPTER SUMMARY

The conditions that gave rise to mass marketing no longer exist. Limited product choice, restricted media options, advertising receptivity and clustered, homogeneous populations have been replaced by their opposites. Those who subscribe to mass marketing assume consumers are homogeneous, the company is the center of the universe, and that it can coerce consumers with advertising puffery delivered at the lowest cost per thousand. But a new way, one that focuses on unique consumers by speaking directly to them with honest communications is poised to take its place. The age of PyroMarketing is set to ignite.

FLASHPOINTS

1. Take an honest look at your advertising. Are you still using mass marketing? Are you still trying to reach *everyone* through undifferentiated media?
2. How are the best customers for your product or service different from the population at large? Make a list. Which of those differences are meaningless and which actually contribute to their purchase decision?
3. Does your current marketing try to serve or sell? Does it treat the consumer like a friend in need of help, or a faceless source of revenue? Imagine yourself as the consumer. How would you like to learn about your company's products? Does your answer resemble your current marketing tactics?

4. What is the cost per thousand of your most recent advertising campaign? What is the cost per customer? How would your advertising tactics change if you shifted your focus from reaching lots of people to reaching precisely the right people?

5. Is your current advertising designed to create interest or appeal to it? Does it try to *make* people thirsty or does it offer a drink to those who already are? How can you make your advertising more relevant? Do you need to change your message? Your audience? Both?

6. Does your advertising make exaggerated claims? Why? Are you worried people won't buy if they know the truth? If you are, then . . .

   a. Maybe your advertising is reaching those who don't need what you're selling. Try telling the truth to an audience that cares. There's nothing wrong with preaching to the choir. The choir will listen.

   b. Perhaps it's time to improve your product or service so that the truth is more impressive than an exaggerated claim.

Fire

Fire is power
—Stephen J. Pyne

When I was young, I read a short story by Jack London titled "To Build a Fire." A classic, it was required reading in my high school English class. It told the story of a character known simply as "the Man." The Man was traveling on foot with his dog through the frozen Canadian wilderness, bound for an old claim on the left fork of Henderson Creek to meet up with "the boys" who were there already.

It was cold when he left, very cold, and also dim since it was still winter and months before the sun would again peek above the horizon, and so he traveled in a perpetual twilight. He was accustomed to the cold but the morning of his journey seemed especially bitter. "He spat speculatively and there was a sharp, explosive crackle that startled him." His spittle had crackled in the air, freezing before hitting the ground. He knew that at fifty below zero spittle would crackle and freeze on the snow, but his had frozen in the air. Even his dog seemed to sense it was too cold to travel and certainly too cold to travel alone. Though he did not know its precise degree, on this morning the temperature was, in fact, seventy-five degrees below zero.

The Man followed the dim trail through the woods and snow along Henderson Creek. Just after his lunch of biscuits and bacon and about halfway to his destination, the Man broke through some thin ice concealed by snow, plunging his legs into the water of a tiny hidden stream, immediately wetting himself halfway to his knees.

He cursed his luck, realizing his misfortune would delay his arrival at camp. At seventy-five degrees below zero, wet clothing was serious. He would have to stop and build a fire to dry out his footgear. He scrambled up the bank of the creek and gathered fuel from the surrounding brush, then set about building his lifesaving fire. "He worked slowly and carefully, keenly aware of his danger." Soon he had built a small fire and was feeding ever-larger twigs and branches into its developing flame. He had saved himself, or so he thought.

Then it happened. He made the mistake of building his fire beneath a spruce tree laden with snow. Each time he snapped a dead limb from its trunk, he agitated the tree and the snow perched precariously on its branches. High up a branch lost its load, triggering a chain reaction that spread throughout the entire tree. Falling snow cascaded from branch to branch until, without warning, it descended upon the man and his fire, and the fire was blotted out!

Shocked and afraid, "as though he had just heard his own death sentence," he scrambled to build another fire. This time, he knew, he must not fail. But now his fingers were frozen and nearly useless. He had exposed them to build his first fire and the cold had drained them of life. He could not feel them, nor will them to move. He gathered material for his

fire by pinching it between the heels of his hands, then drop-
ping it into a pile before him. But this would not work for
striking a match. Through great difficulty he was able to place
a single match between his teeth and to light it after scratch-
ing it many times across his pant leg. But, as it lit, he inhaled
the sulfur smoke from the match, coughed violently, and
extinguished its flame.

Since he could not hold a single match with his useless
fingers, he caught the whole bunch in the heels of his hands
and scratched them along his legs until it flared into flame.
He pressed them toward a scrap of birch bark to begin his
fire. The flame lapped at his hands and he could smell his
burning flesh and feel the slightest sensation of pain beginning deep within his hands. The pain grew until he could bear
it no longer and he dropped the bunch of matches into the
snow where they extinguished with a sizzle. But the birch
bark was alight!

He cherished the flame and nurtured it by clumsily adding
bits of fuel. But the lack of feeling and control in his hands
meant he could not pick and choose what to add. He fed it with
tiny twigs and dry grass, but also with moss and dirt. A large
piece of green moss fell onto his tiny fire, disrupting its nucleus.
Bits of burning twigs and leaves were scattered and one by one
they breathed a tiny puff of smoke and went out.

Panicked, the Man thought of running the remaining distance to camp and the boys and the fire they must have built.
He rose and ran, but lacked the endurance to run the long distance and soon fell. He rose and ran again, but again he fell.
The third time he fell he realized the frost was extending from
his hands and feet, creeping into the rest of his body. He
endured his final panic and decided to meet death with dig-
nity. He sat in the snow, drifted off to sleep, and to his death.

A WAY TO LOOK AT MARKETING

Some years ago I had a startling revelation. I am the Man in Jack London's story. In fact, if you are responsible for selling or marketing a product or service of any kind, you are too. I doubt Jack London knew it as he wrote, but he was describing the situation faced by every modern businessperson and, in the process, providing a way to think about marketing—a metaphor that, if heeded, can dramatically improve your effectiveness while simplifying your task.

If a picture is worth a thousand words, then a metaphor is worth a thousand pictures. It can help us understand the new or unfamiliar by comparing it with what we already know. Metaphors package ideas, making them easier to remember and apply.

EVERY MARKETER . . .
1. Is lost in the freezing wilderness
2. Must start a fire to survive
3. Has only one match

LOST IN THE FREEZING WILDERNESS

Maybe you've chosen marketing, but more likely it has chosen you. Whether you have crash-landed in the wilderness and must find your way out; are a small-business owner forced to market your company or watch it fail, or a longtime marketing professional who has voluntarily stepped into the rough country because you love the challenge—your task is the same. If you are going to survive, then you must be prepared.

Preparation begins by embracing the reality of your challenge. The Man died because he didn't appreciate the seriousness of the situation, the difficulty of his task, or the limitation of his resources. The Man stepped boldly into the wilderness just as he had many times before. He believed the approach that had worked previously would serve him again. He was experienced, after all. He knew how to survive, or so he thought. In the story a character named the Old-Timer warns the Man not to travel alone when temperature dips past fifty below. While such advice made sense for the Old-Timer, the Man didn't think it applied to a young, healthy, experienced adventurer like him. His previous successes and a pocket full of matches filled him with false confidence but ultimately failed him. While the Man slept, things had changed. Though he didn't realize it, he awoke to a new day, one much colder than any he had previously known. For this journey, the old way of building a fire—the way that worked so well just the day before—no longer applied.

Though fifty degrees below zero was cold—even cold enough to kill—the temperature was not fifty below. The temperature was seventy-five degrees below zero. Fifty degrees below zero may have allowed two attempts to build a fire. Seventy-five below meant only one. At that temperature he could not rely on former ways.

It's tempting to think there's little practical difference between the two—both are so cold and foreign to our experience. But we know well the difference between fifty and seventy five degrees above zero. It's the difference between a coat and shorts, between football and golf. Even the difference of a single degree can be profound as 211 degrees Fahrenheit and 212 degrees Fahrenheit illustrate. Preparations for hot water will not accommodate steam.

Your success, like the Man's, depends on an honest, accurate, and thorough evaluation of your circumstances and your plans. It's not enough to concede that "it's tough out there." That's the same as admitting that fifty below zero is cold. You must honestly consider your situation, the opportunities it presents, and the corresponding limitations. It's not enough to repeat former plans. Advertising will not drive sales simply because you need it to, any more than a fire will start because your life depends on it. Consider the challenge faced by this book.

Each year between 120,000 and 150,000 new books are published in the United States. Last year 5,301 of those titles were business books, a 30 percent increase from the year before.[1] They join a library of 3.2 million books already in print. To put this in perspective, it helps to realize that a typical Barnes and Noble superstore accommodates only about 110,000 titles, or between 10,000 and 40,000 fewer than just the *new* books published each year. If there are about 56,000 business books in print, and assuming an average cost of approximately $20, that means individual business titles sell only about 323 copies per year—and yet my publisher and I expect my book to sell many times more. Welcome to my wilderness. Brrrrrrrrrrrrrr.

The challenge is daunting, and yet the business book market hit $828.6 million this year and some business titles sell millions of copies. People are buying them. The trick is to understand the process and their motivations. No one steps through the front door of a Barnes and Noble and, after drawing the smell of books and coffee deeply into their lungs, determines, "Today I'm going to buy me a book and I don't much care which one." People aren't like that. They care deeply about certain books and not the least about others. So, who are these people? How do they discover new books? Why do they choose the ones they do? What kind of person will choose mine, and why? Questions like these lead to a sobering appreciation for the brutality of the wilderness but also to successful survival plans.

YOU MUST START A FIRE TO SURVIVE

Your task, like the Man's, is to start a fire. Starting a fire means selling your product or service. This is all that really matters. It's the only way to generate revenue and pursuing anything else is a mistake.

Many small businesses intuitively know this. Their budgets are tiny and their margins are tight. Marketing must deliver sales, and fast. But larger firms are sometimes lulled into complacency. In those cases marketers can obsess over all the wrong things. As if ascending a business version of Maslow's hierarchy of needs, they abandon fundamental necessities like sales to pursue a sort-of corporate self-actualization. They spend millions chasing awareness or mind-share or, worst of all, advertising awards. But what good does it do? People may pay attention, but attention doesn't pay. Cancer has awareness, but nobody wants it. Stock prices don't rise or fall on quarterly "mind share" reports, and advertising awards do not pay the bills or fetch much on eBay should times turn tough. Awareness, mind-share, even branding, are the *result* of sales and should be secondary, if you pursue them at all. Seeking them first is like saying, I'll build my fire after I warm up. But, if you don't build your fire—if your marketing does not produce sales—you won't ever warm up. What you need are sales and everything else, including awareness, mind-share and branding, will follow.

Branding is all the rage these days, but I think it's overvalued and badly misunderstood. A study by NPD Group found that almost half of those who described themselves as highly loyal to a brand didn't feel that way even one year later.[2] Another study, according to James Surowiecki writing in *Wired*, "found that only four percent of consumers would be willing to stick with a brand if its competitors offered a better value at the same price."[3] What's the point of building a new brand or defending an established one through advertising if the consumer's brand loyalty is so fleeting? In a market filled with promiscuous consumers it's better to pursue sales.

It's comforting to think that advertising builds your brand. If it did, then you could control what people thought about your company and products, deftly manipulating their perceptions with each new campaign. In a perfect world this might be true, but this is the wilderness and things don't work that way. All brands—including yours—exist only in the mind of the consumer. The customer defines it. You don't. What's more, customers characterize your brand based primarily on their experience with your product or service, not their encounters with your advertising. Consumers see through the mask. Brand advertising, it turns out, only brands your advertising.

The most important factor when making a purchase decision isn't advertising. According to a Roper survey, more Americans (71 percent) list "past experience with a brand" as the primary factor in their decision.[4] That figure rose to an astounding 88 percent among the most important class of consumer—those most likely to influence other shoppers' purchases. Experience is how you influence the consumer and those people whose opinions they most respect. Advertising often exaggerates. Experience can't. Your business, therefore, is defined by what it actually delivers, not by the promises of its advertising. Brands are more like the shadow cast by the image your company and its products create. To alter your brand you must change the shape of the company and products casting the shadow. Take Firestone, for example.

When Firestone tires were blamed for causing rollover accidents involving Ford Explorers, the company recalled and replaced six and a half million tires. It also ran a print advertising campaign with the headline "We'll Make It Right" in which it touted its commitment to safety and pleaded with consumers to trust its tires.[5] Which, do you think, had a more profound affect on Firestone's brand in the mind of the consumer, its advertising or the experience of barrel-rolling through the median after a blowout? For many Firestone tire owners the message of its advertising didn't match their experience with the product. What they actually delivered, not what they promised, defined them.

Even mildly disappointing product experiences can have a profound impact on the strongest of brands. In 2002, Interbrand declared Nokia the sixth most valuable brand in the world and valued it at $30 billion. But Nokia failed to make the clamshell-style cell phones consumers preferred and within one year Nokia lost $6 billion in equity amid tumbling sales.[6] A strong brand name had not sustained sales of an inferior product. Instead, outdated product designs eroded a once-powerful brand.

For Firestone or Nokia, or anyone else, the quickest way to build your brand is to build your sales and the only way to build a *good* brand is to build a *good* product.

But, even if you've made sales your goal, it's not enough to simply place advertising. Don't confuse activity with accomplishment. Remember, the Man also lit matches. Your promotional activity must lead as directly as possible to sales just as the matches you light must lead to a fire. Many old habits will die along the way. But don't worry, PyroMarketing will help you choose tactics that deliver results.

YOU HAVE ONLY ONE MATCH

Picturing a single match is a reminder of the finite nature of your marketing resources. No matter what they are—money, people, or time—you only have so much. Opportunity costs are critical. How will you use your match? What will you touch it to? What tactics will deliver results? Use it wisely by building your marketing fire according to proven principles. You may only get one chance.

METAPHORS

I love metaphors and my mind is constantly searching for analogies to help me understand and explain the world around me. Over the years I've heard the various comparisons applied to the marketing process. In the water metaphor consumers swam in a sea of advertising, soaking up messages from saturation campaigns. Marketing as warfare was another popular idea. Campaigns targeted consumers with shotgun or rifle approaches. The competition was the enemy. Guerrilla marketing was a thrifty variation that "tilted the balance of power" so that smaller companies could battle against rival superpowers using unconventional techniques. More recently the idea of marketing as a viral contagion has been going around. In this view the marketing message is a virus spread from person to person like the common cold.

Each idea had its merits but also its problems. None of them fit exactly. The water metaphor was self-absorbed because it focused too much on the advertiser. The marketer always made the rain. It didn't provide for the consumer's role in receiving or spreading the message. Where, I wondered, was word of mouth?

I never did understand the warfare metaphor. If the competition was the enemy, why were we shooting our customers?

I liked the contagion idea much more. At least it explained

the consumer's contribution to the marketing process. But it was too haphazard. Some people "caught" the message while others didn't. It seemed as if casual contact, or perhaps even failing to wash your hands, might govern the marketing process. It allowed that certain people are better at spreading a disease, but ignored the fact that some prospects are also much more susceptible to catching it.

Despite their shortcomings, these metaphors really did improve my understanding and practice of marketing, though they failed to account for all of the forces I saw at work in promotional campaigns. The missing elements were too important to ignore.

1. Advertising can't *make* people buy. It exerts an influence, but it isn't irresistible. Some people buy an advertised product, while others don't. Why?
2. The likelihood a consumer will respond to advertising seems proportional to their interest in the product or service. As a result, people who respond well to promotions for one item may ignore marketing for something else.
3. Advertising has limitations. It works with those most likely to buy, but lacks the persuasive power to convince everyone else, no matter how many exposures you subject them to.
4. The personal recommendation of a friend or family member is the most influential marketing force. But people don't recommend indiscriminately. When a product thrills them, they recommend it to select people, picking and choosing those they believe will enjoy it most.
5. Customer evangelists are not created equal. Some people recommend more often and more effectively than others. And, even among those who tell their friends to buy, cer-

tain people's recommendations are more effective than others'.

6. Popularity begets popularity. As more people embrace a product, service, or brand, the more it seems other people are willing to adopt it too. But this process depends on proximity. People can be affected by an emerging trend only if they can see it emerge, and to see it emerge, they must have points of contact that connected communities provide. When that occurs, then the marketing process that started the trend gives way to some other force as the movement advances, propelled, it seems, by its own inertia.

For years, I used the old metaphors, variously drenching, shooting, or infecting prospects for my products and enjoying modest success. But along the way I kept my eyes and ears open, searching for an idea that captured the useful portions of existing metaphors while accommodating the missing elements. I searched, that is, until the day I discovered fire.

FIRE

Fire is, arguably, mankind's greatest discovery. Harnessing its power has transformed our lives. It heats our homes, generates our electricity, propels our automobiles, and it provides a metaphor that can transform the way we think about the marketing process. But before we can appreciate the many ways it parallels marketing, it's necessary to explore the science of fire to a greater degree.

From the kitchen stove to the backyard grill, we are surrounded by fire. Rarely, however, do we stop to consider just what it is or how it operates. Fire is a complex combination of chemical and physical reactions and its behavior responds to

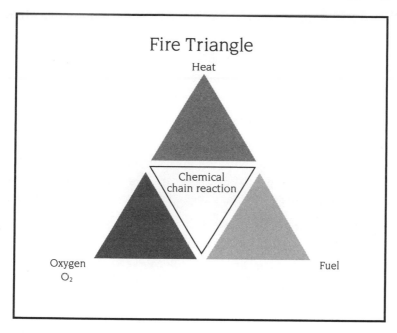

Figure 2.1 Fire Triangle. Fire requires fuel, oxygen, heat, and the heat released during the combustion reaction.

a vast array of variables. Fire, like marketing, can be quite complex. But, when reduced to its essence, it can also be quite simple and that simplicity can, in turn, help us understand marketing more clearly.

According to *Essentials of Fire Fighting*, a training manual developed by the International Fire Service Training Association (IFSTA): "Combustion is the self-sustaining process of rapid oxidation of a fuel, which produces heat and light. Fire is the result of a rapid combustion reaction."[7] Technically speaking, then, "fire" describes the result, not the process. The process is called combustion. But that's splitting hairs. You probably use the words "fire" and "combustion" interchangeably. To keep things simple, I will too.

There are four essential ingredients to every fire. They are:

1. Fuel
2. Oxygen
3. Heat
4. Heat from the chemical reaction

Fire is impossible without all four and a fire, no matter how furious, will sputter and die if deprived of any one of them. Together they form what's called the "fire triangle." (see Figure 2.1). It provides a convenient way to symbolize the elements of fire and their codependent relationship.

Fire occurs when electrons released from fuel join with oxygen in the surrounding air. This rapid oxidation is a chemical reaction called combustion. The oxidation reaction is quite common and involves everything from rusting metal to the way our bodies metabolize food. What makes combustion unique is its speed. Rust is slow. Combustion is frantic.

Energy is stored in the fuel's molecular bonds. But those bonds are very strong. The fuel's electrons, for the most part, prefer to remain right where they are. But when fuel is heated, its molecules, along with oxygen molecules in the atmosphere, become active. As energy is transferred to the fuel, its electrons begin to orbit farther and farther from the nucleus. The more the fuel is heated, the more active its molecules become until they eclipse the ignition point. At this moment the bonds suddenly sever, releasing electrons from their orbit, and the fuel ignites. In a chemical jailbreak, freed electrons rush away from the fuel and join, instead, with oxygen from the surrounding air. As they do, the reaction gives off light and vast amounts of additional heat, which, in turn, perpetuates the reaction. Heat is the energy output of fire. It transfers to nearby fuel, raising its temperature and setting it alight, in a chain reaction that causes the fire to spread.[8]

MARKETING FIRE

One day I realized that marketing had a great deal in common with the combustion process and that fire might provide the marketing metaphor I had been searching for. But metaphors often break down under close scrutiny. Things stop matching up or analogies are stretched to improbable extremes to make them fit. I was worried the comparison with fire might suffer the same problems. But the more I learned about fire, the better marketing metaphor it became. Every element in the fire triangle—every force in the chemical reaction—corresponded to the marketing process. It even accounted for the elements missing from the old metaphors. Thousands of years after man had discovered fire, I discovered PyroMarketing and this is how it works.

In the PyroMarketing reaction, consumers are the fuel. There is money stored in their wallets, but there is also a very strong bond between consumers and their money. They won't give it up easily. Marketing provides the activation energy that starts the reaction. Heated by promotions, consumers become more excited. When their level of excitement eclipses their purchase threshold—the consumer's equivalent to a fuel's ignition point—the bond to their money breaks and they exchange it for the promoted product, or what I call "Oh![2]." Oh![2] refers to the product and is to PyroMarketing what oxygen (O_2) is to fire. But, like oxygen, its concentrations vary according to how remarkable the consumers find your product or service. Finally, when consumers are thrilled by their purchase, their temperature increases. They become enthusi-

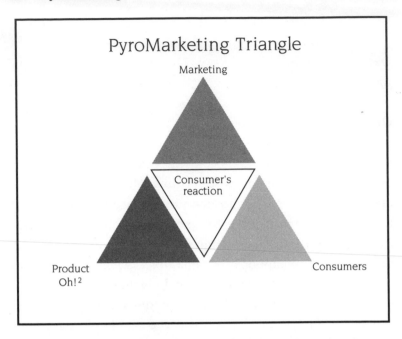

Figure 2.2 PyroMarketing Triangle. This new method requires consumers, product (Oh!²), marketing, and a positive consumer reaction.

astic evangelists who recommend it to their friends and family. If the product disappoints them, they cool. The consumers' reaction is like the combustion reaction and provides the energy output that either spreads or extinguishes the fire. Interested consumers, a remarkable product, effective marketing, and the positive reaction of satisfied customers are the four essential ingredients to a PyroMarketing campaign. You cannot market without all four, and a campaign, no matter how successful, will sputter and die if deprived of any one of them.

Let's look more closely at each element of fire and its PyroMarketing counterpart.

O$_2$

Oxygen is the life breath of fire. The more vigorous a fire, the more oxygen it needs. The air we breathe is about 22 percent oxygen and provides an ample supply to most fires. If oxygen content slips below 18 percent, however, combustion begins to slow, the fire struggles, and its temperature plummets. Anything less than 15 percent is suffocating and won't support fire at all. It is not enough, then, to say that fire requires oxygen. Fire needs oxygen in concentrations above 15 percent and in amounts equal to the fire's demand. Likewise, Pyro-Marketing needs more than just a product or service. It can flourish and grow only when nourished by *remarkable* products and *exceptional* services.

In PyroMarketing, Oh!^{2} represents a remarkable product. When consumers' experience with your product or service delivers more than they expected, they are doubly satisfied. They become customer evangelists who exponentially increase the power of your marketing through enthusiastic word of mouth. If it's great, they'll find out in a hurry and tell their friends. But, be warned, PyroMarketing exposes inferior products with equal speed. If your product disappoints, then no amount of marketing heat can save it and PyroMarketing will only kill it more quickly.

In 1975, Hollywood thought it had stumbled upon the secret formula for brewing a blockbuster. *Jaws* opened and within two months became the most successful film in history. Traditionally, Hollywood had launched movies slowly with a process known as platforming. It would open a film at a few theaters and broaden its distribution over a period of weeks and months only after it proved popular in those test markets. But *Jaws* was different. It opened on four hundred screens, more than any previous film, following what *Times* critic Stephen Farber called an "aggressive media blitz" that included the largest national prime-time television advertising campaign ever employed for a film. Farber believed that moviegoers had been manipulated by the film's marketing—"pummeled" into submission and into theaters. He thought that heat alone could sustain a fire. Simultaneously overestimating the power of promotions, underestimating the importance of the consumer, and ignoring the remarkable nature of the film altogether, he wrote: "Audiences who think they made *Jaws* a success are pitifully naïve about the mass media."[9]

But who was naive? Repeating a formula should duplicate its result, yet in the years since *Jaws* Hollywood has been unable to consistently replicate its success, despite applying its formula to countless would-be blockbusters. *The Hulk*, for example, opened in 4,000 theaters but was playing on only 600 screens within five weeks. Between the first and second weekend, its revenues collapsed by 70 percent! Expansive distribution and tens of millions of dollars in marketing could not overcome a remarkably unremarkable product. Without Oh![2] *The Hulk* was quickly smothered.

It's not that the *Jaws* formula of broad distribution and mass marketing no longer applies; it's more accurate to say that it never really did. "*Jaws* may have opened big because Universal marketed it well and released it widely," wrote James Surowiecki, on The Financial Page of *The New Yorker,* "But it stayed big because people liked it."[10] If anything, that's the formula. A detailed study of two thousand movies recently conducted by economists Arthur De Vany and W. David Walls found that the only real predictor of long-term success is word of mouth. "After a movie opens," they wrote, "the audience decides its fate."[11]

The same was true for *The Purpose-Driven® Life*. Its astonishing success was due, in part, to the remarkable nature of the product itself. It wasn't merely a good read. When readers were asked about the book's impact in a survey conducted two years after its release, their most common response was, "It changed my life."[12]

Readers decided its fate by elevating *The Purpose-Driven® Life* onto the *USA Today* bestseller list where, as of this writing, it has spent 107 weeks! Over that period many other books have come and gone. None of the 10 best-selling hardcover nonfiction titles on the list the day *The Purpose-Driven® Life* first appeared is still among the top 150. Other books, like *Living History* by Hillary Rodham Clinton and *The Glorious*

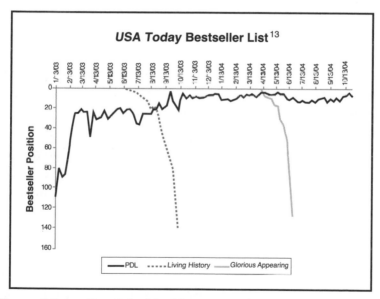

Figure 2.3 A nation full of fuel (consumers) and ample heat (marketing) could not sustain the sales of *Living History* or *The Glorious Appearing*. Without Oh!² they quickly vanished from the list.

Appearing, the final book in the Left Behind series, debuted at higher positions amid a flurry of promotion and publicity then quickly faltered. But the remarkable nature of *PDL* enabled its success to endure. Figure 2.3 compares the best-seller positions of *Living History* and *The Glorious Appearing* with *The Purpose-Driven® Life*.

"You're either remarkable or invisible," wrote best-selling business author Seth Godin in *Purple Cow;* "the only route to healthy growth is a remarkable product."[14] Trying to grow your sales without it is like trying to build a fire in a vacuum.

IGNITION POINT

Fire begins when a fuel's temperature passes its ignition point. That's the temperature above which it will burn without the application of additional heat. Like water freezing at 32 degrees Fahrenheit or boiling at 212 degrees, a fuel's ignition temperature is a strict and critically important boundary. Below this temperature, fuel will not burn. Above it, fuel burns, and will continue burning even if you remove the heat that originally started the fire. Think of birthday candles. You hold a lit match to the candle until its temperature surpasses the ignition point. Once it is lit, it continues to burn and you can blow out your match because combustion is a chain reaction. Once you start a fire, it persists on its own until it is deprived of fuel or oxygen, the reaction is interrupted, or its heat falls below the fuel's ignition temperature.

Ignition temperatures vary widely depending on the fuel. A temperature that lights one material may not ignite others. At 806 degrees the pages of this book will burn, but at 800 degrees they won't. You'll need 932 degrees to light a Douglas fir and 1,112 degrees before natural gas will combust. Nothing less will do. Country singer Jerry Reed was right when he sang, "When you're hot, you're hot. When you're not, you're not."

There is almost nothing that won't burn given sufficient heat. Here are the ignition temperatures for several common materials. Notice how widely they vary.

FUEL	IGNITION TEMP F°[15]
Peat	441
Match heads	518
Wood	572
Bituminous Coal	572
Pages of this book	806
Propane	896
Douglas fir (shavings)	932
Natural gas	1,112

You don't need a flame or even a spark to start a fire. Oxygen, fuel, and enough heat to push that fuel past its ignition point are all that is required. The California Department of Forestry and Fire Protection advises residents to protect their property from an approaching wildfire by closing shutters and heavy drapes and taking down sheer curtains that might combust.[16] At first this might seem a little like rearranging deck chairs on the *Titanic*, but this advice can be the difference between a close call and disaster. That is because radiant heat from the passing fire can ignite curtains on the inside of a closed window though no flame or spark ever touches them. Closing shutters and heavy drapes may spare the house from destruction by blocking radiant heat that might have ignited materials with lower ignition temperatures.

Consumers have widely varying ignition temperatures too. They are not equally susceptible to your marketing because one person's purchase threshold can be so much higher than another's. Some light easily while others remain virtually fireproof. This is a key element to PyroMarketing and a fatal omission from all other marketing metaphors. People are different and those differences make them more or less likely to buy your product. By identifying those with the lowest ignition temperatures, you can use them to start your fire. And, because the heat released as a fuel burns is often greater than the heat needed to ignite it, tiny marketing budgets can start fires that grow to immense proportions.

HEAT BALANCE

"What's inside that warehouse?" is the urgent first question of a firefighter arriving at the scene of an industrial blaze. That's because how fast the fire will grow and how large it will eventually become depend on the heat energy released by the burning fuel.[17] The heat release rate (HRR) measures the heat output from a fire over a period of time. It reveals the fire's "horsepower" and can be measured in Btu or, British thermal units. A Btu is the amount of energy required to raise the temperature of one pound of water, one degree Fahrenheit.[18] The total energy released by the fire over a period of time is its heat release rate.

HRR is the driving force for fire and the single most important variable in describing one. If the heat output is high, then the fire will advance, growing in size and intensity. Of the four elements necessary for fire, heat is unique because it is the only ingredient that a fire can make itself. Fuel doesn't make more fuel. Oxygen cannot make more oxygen, but a fire can grow to enormous proportions because *heat makes more heat.*

But just how much heat it will make depends on the fuel. Like ignition temperature, heat release rates also vary widely from one material to the next. Some materials burn cool while others burn hot. Even seemingly similar fuels can have vastly different heat release characteristics. Take your Christmas tree, for example.

Each year about two hundred house fires in the United States begin with a Christmas tree.[19] Whether your family's gifts are stacked beneath a Scotch pine or a spruce could determine the extent of the fire and whether or not you'll even have a home for the holidays. Scotch pines burn hot, with an HRR of 1,800 to 5,000 Btu/second, whereas spruce trees burn much cooler at between 500 and 650 Btu/second. Because of its lower HRR, your family would have time to extinguish a fire in a spruce before additional damage was done. But if you have a Scotch pine, you may watch in horror as within moments its more intense heat ignites the sofa. The sofa meanwhile, with its foam cushions and an HRR of more than 3,000 Btu/second, would quickly involve the rest of the living room, lighting walls and adjacent furniture and forcing your family to evacuate. As you watched from the front yard, your minivan, still parked in the garage, would burst into flames searing nearby bikes and garden tools with an astounding 8,000-plus Btu/second released by its many plastic components.

It's easy to see why heat release rate is so important to the growth of the fire. It is equally important to marketing; just as people's ignition temperatures vary, their heat release rates differ too. Some people try a product or service and may casually mention it to a friend or neighbor. Others, however, "burn hot" and make it their life's mission to tell others about their good experience, quickly igniting everyone around them. Whether a customer evangelist burns hot depends on their satisfaction with your product or service. The more thrilling their experience, the hotter they will burn. But apathy to disappointment will leave them lukewarm to cool. Once again *The Purpose-Driven® Life* provides a fascinating insight.

Some time after its release we surveyed consumers who had purchased the book. We knew something profound was at work when more than thirty thousand people responded to the survey, but we were still unprepared for what they told us. We learned that 83 percent of the people who bought the book were actively recommending it to others. What's more, nearly 47 percent bought additional copies of the $20 book and gave them away. Seventy-three percent of that group gave away one to three copies, 17 percent gave away four to six, and an astounding 7 percent bought ten or more copies and gave them away! The book had changed their life, and their high heat release rate made them a dramatically more powerful force than advertising and the single greatest contributor to the book's explosive growth.

But, for all their importance, traditional mass marketing often ignores customer evangelists. A mass marketing approach would reason that the best prospects for *The Purpose-Driven® Life* were people who hadn't yet bought it. But Zondervan's research suggested something dramatically different. The best prospect for *The Purpose-Driven® Life* was *the person who already owned a copy.* Not only would they willingly recommend it to strangers, but also about half of them were willing to buy between one and ten more! Customer evangelists had gone beyond simply telling others about the book; they were actually buying and distributing additional copies! The key to igniting new prospects for *The Purpose-Driven® Life* was not tossing matches on new markets; it was fanning the flames of existing customer evangelists.

HEAT BALANCE

While a material's heat release rate is important to a fire, its physical orientation matters too because of a trait called radiative feedback.

Suppose you build a tiny fire comprised of three twigs and then separate them. One by one they will go out. When they were burning as a group, they shared radiative feedback. The heat from the first twig sent energy to the second and third, helping to sustain their combustion reaction. Likewise, heat from twigs two and three contributed to the first twig's fire. When combustion from the various fuels feeds heat back to a fire causing its temperature to rise, a blaze is said to have a "positive heat balance."[20] A positive heat balance is what causes a fire to grow.

Separate the twigs, however, and things change dramatically. Deprived of shared heat, each twig must survive on its own. All are thrust into a negative heat balance, a sort of thermal poverty where, without the energy from nearby reactions, heat dissipates faster than it can be generated and the temperature of each twig slowly falls. The poor get poorer, until the temperature slips below the ignition point and each fire goes out.

There is strength in numbers for marketing as well. Bestselling books rise and fashion trends emerge from communities of like-minded people clustered so that the heat of their excitement is easily shared. Popular movies and trendy music are propelled up the charts by the same force. A teenager who plays her iPod for friends at the mall releases more promotional heat than a monthlong television advertising campaign.

In the 1960s, network television formed the hub of such networks by organizing most of the population around two or three popular programs. Mass media unified a disconnected public. Today, though, Internet chat rooms, message boards, social networks, urban tribes, local churches, and coffee shops are where people gather to commune with friends and stoke their common interests.

It is not enough to reach isolated people with your marketing message. If you want your fire to grow, then you must create a positive heat balance by organizing customers and prospects into communities where they can renew their passion and interest by sharing heat with others.

PHASES OF FIRE

Fires, like marketing campaigns, evolve through phases. The three phases of a fire are: the incipient phase, the steady-state burning phase, and the hot-smoldering phase. The incipient phase is the earliest and begins with the actual ignition. At this point, combustion is limited to the materials that first caught fire, let's say the Christmas tree in the living room. The reaction is producing some heat from its flame, but the temperature of the room is relatively unchanged. That heat, however, will increase as the fire progresses.

In the steady-state burning phase ample fuel, oxygen, and the heat of the reaction allow the fire to grow to a point where total involvement is possible. The fire is burning freely now as smoke and flames from its reaction superheat the surrounding air igniting adjacent materials like a couch or an end table. As long as there is sufficient oxygen, the fire will continue to grow. It is during the steady-state burning phase that flashover can take place.

Flashover occurs when the contents of the room are gradually heated to their ignition point causing everything to spontaneously combust. In an instant, fire flashes over the entire space as the living room and all of its contents explode into flame. During its early stages, a fire spreads only at its edge, making it easy to predict how and where it will grow. Flashover, by contrast, is dramatic and occurs with few visual cues. As walls and furniture invisibly pass their ignition point, they suddenly ignite and a fire that has involved only the Christmas tree, an end table, and a sofa instantly engulfs the entire room.

The hot-smoldering phase is the third and final stage. Here there may be no flames at all as burning is reduced to glowing embers. A fresh supply of oxygen can renew the flames, but without it the fire will eventually burn out.

In many ways this process is similar to the way new products diffuse through markets. As an innovation is launched, heat from its marketing plan ignites a small group of consumers most receptive to the innovation. During this early phase they may be the only ones buying or using it. But, over time, and especially if they can share their enthusiasm with a like-minded group, they become more excited and begin to tell others. The heat they generate is greater than the marketing that started the process and enables the fire to grow. The confluence of product, eager consumers, and the heat from their positive reaction, spreads the fire as other groups adopt the innovation. The more popular it becomes, the more new people adopt it. Heat generates more heat until the market reaches flashover. Eventually, the process matures and the fire dies.

CAMPFIRES AND MARKETING PLANS

Steve Honsinger can start a fire in the wilderness without matches or a lighter and he can do it in 8.67 seconds! Steve is a builder by trade, but as a hobby he enjoys reenacting "rendezvous," historical events spanning the mid eighteenth century to the late nineteenth. Dressed in period attire and camping in tents and teepees, participants vie for prizes at archery ranges, tomahawk-throwing contests, by target shooting with muzzle-loading rifles, and by quickly starting fires using flint and steel. The best can do it in two seconds or less.

To start a campfire this way you need a flint, an iron, tinder, charred cloth, and wood ranging from shavings to logs. Preparation is the key. Steve begins by fashioning what looks like a small bird's nest of tinder by unraveling strands of burlap. The filaments are finer than hair and ignite easily. Next he presses a piece of charred cloth into the center of the tinder nest. Charred cloth is just that, a piece of cotton fabric partially charred by fire.

To start the fire, Steve sharply strikes flint against his iron. The stone shaves red-hot pieces from the metal in a shower of sparks that he catches in the charred cloth cradled in the hollow of the tinder. When a good spark lands, he sets down his flint and iron. Picking up the nest of tinder, he brings it near his face and blows strongly onto the sparks. The sparks shine brightly as a glowing ring expands around it, spreading like a halo in the charred cloth. As it does, Steve folds the package of tinder and charred cloth in half like a taco, forcing the two sides of the glowing ring nearer each other to share the increasing heat. Steve holds the package closer to his mouth and continues to blow. Almost immediately it bursts into flame, instantly involving the jute twine tinder. At once Steve drops the flaming tinder to the ground and feeds fine wood shavings and paraffin to the developing flame. The ignition temperature of wood shavings was beyond the reach of the sparks that lit the tinder, but they catch quickly on the open flame and sustain his fire. With the wood shavings lit, Steve removes the tinder and stamps out its flame with his moccasin before returning it to his fire kit. He'll use it to start his next fire. Gradually Steve feeds twigs and kindling onto the fire. As it grows, he eventually adds the logs that will maintain his fire into the night. Lost in the freezing wilderness, Steve Honsinger could build a lifesaving fire with a single spark. He understands the science of combustion and uses it to his advantage.

As we will see in the next four chapters, successful marketing plans are built the same way. Your fate in the freezing wilderness depends on your ability to gather the driest tinder, touch it with the match, fan the flames, and save the coals.

CHAPTER SUMMARY

Every marketer is like the Man in "To Build a Fire" by Jack London. Lost in the freezing marketplace, you must sell your product or service to survive. With limited marketing resources you must succeed on your very first attempt because you may not get a second. If you think of marketing as fire, you can do it. Consumers are like fuel. There is money stored in their wallets, but there is also a very strong bond between consumers and their money. Marketing is the heat that raises them beyond their ignition temperature and sets them alight. Consumers exchange their money for products or services, the equivalent of oxygen to a fire. The more remarkable consumers find your product, the higher its concentration of Oh!². The more satisfied consumers are with your product or service, the higher their heat release rate and this positive word of mouth is the single most important factor in the growth of your marketing fire. Building communities of satisfied customers helps them increase their excitement by sharing their experiences. This radiative feedback contributes to a positive heat balance transforming simple customers into customer evangelists who grow your marketing fire to flashover.

FLASHPOINTS

1. When was the last time you checked the temperature? Things may have changed. Make a thorough, honest evaluation of the marketplace and your business and prepare accordingly.
2. Is your marketing designed to start a fire? Is it tightly focused on sales? Or are you wasting your one match chasing awareness, hoping it will lead to sales? What would happen if you devoted all of it to generating sales instead?
3. How do consumers react to your product or service? Have you ever asked, Does it have Oh!²? You can't build a fire unless it does. What changes would improve people's reaction?
4. Describe the consumer with the lowest ignition temperature relative to your product or service. Is that who you currently target with your marketing?
5. Does your marketing reach people when they are clustered into groups so that they can better share your message and their excitement through radiative feedback? Or are you using mass advertising tactics that reach people in isolation where their enthusiasm cools and dies?
6. If you had to build a fire in the wilderness with one match and could choose among fuels that included dry tinder, tiny twigs, sticks, logs, and wet leaves, which materials would you use and when? Think about the people you target with your marketing. Have you prioritized them properly?

3

Gather the Driest Tinder

. . . consider what a great forest is set on fire by a small spark.
—James 3:5 NIV

POINT OF ORIGIN

Every fire has a point of origin. So does every trend, every fad, every social epidemic, and every best-selling product. Arson investigators look for the point of origin when probing for the cause of a fire. It is also where successful marketing campaigns begin.

Movements like those fueling the popularity of *The Passion of the Christ* or *The Purpose-Driven® Life* don't happen everywhere at once. They aren't begun by blanketing millions with mass advertising. By the time most people become aware of such phenomena, they are already wildly popular and so it seems they always have been. People take for granted that anything so big was never small. But such phenomena do start small—sometimes with just a few people—and then they grow. Indeed it is impossible to start them any other way.

The Bear Fire in north-central California began when a lawn mower blade struck a rock and a single spark ignited explosively dry grasses in an area south of Shasta Lake. From that point of origin the fire grew, eventually blackening 9,922 acres and destroying eighty homes, thirty outbuildings, and ten vehicles.[1] That one spark would have cooled and died had it landed almost anywhere else. Had it struck nearly any of the objects it eventually burned—homes, garages, cars, trees and shrubs—nothing would have happened. The blaze occurred because a single spark didn't land on those things. By chance it landed on a wisp of dry grass that was ready to burn. It settled on fuel whose ignition temperature was so low that the energy from a single spark was more than enough to set it ablaze. It landed on the driest tinder.

The heat released by that burning wisp of grass ignited neighboring blades, which, in turn, lit twigs and sticks, which lit whole trees, and so on. The fire began small and it grew. With each step it spread, gaining power and momentum. Fanned by breezes, each new stage released more heat, and as the temperature increased in degree, the fire could ignite new materials. It was already quite large by the time people in other parts of the country became aware of it through news coverage, but it did not start that way. The blaze that charred thousands of acres was the culmination of a single spark.

Fashion trends, best-selling books, wildly popular movies, in fact all social phenomena, behave this way. Given the proper conditions, they may grow to enormous proportions, but they all start with the driest tinder, the people most likely to buy.

WET LEAVES

Coveting the wrong consumers is a trap that has caught marketing people for years. There are millions of people who don't want what you sell. They will never buy your product or service. You can't make them, and you shouldn't try. So forget about them. Immediately!

No product or service in history has appealed to everyone, and yours won't be the first. This is a fundamental truth. The sooner you embrace it, the sooner you will be freed to sell your product or service to the millions and millions of people who *will* buy.

Bill Laimbeer, the center for the Detroit Pistons during their championship years in the late 1980s and early 1990s, was loved by Pistons fans and loathed by everyone else. Fans in opposing arenas saved their most virulent booing for his introduction and peppered him with catcalls throughout the game. He loved it. A reporter asked him about this during an interview: "Doesn't it bother you that fans in other arenas hate you?" "I don't need a million friends," he replied.

Bill Laimbeer was right! He knew he couldn't perform at the highest level for the Detroit Pistons *and* win the admiration of opposing fans. To try would be to fail at both. Was it possible for them to hate him less? Maybe. But it meant compromising his primary duty—dominating for the Detroit Pistons.

Don't covet people unlikely to buy. You can't start your fire with wet leaves. Yet many foolishly try. They compromise their product, reducing its appeal to the primary buyer, in a futile attempt to lure less likely consumers. It happens all the time in publishing. The author of a book targeting women demands a less feminine cover "so it won't exclude men." But many times the very quality that attracts one group alienates another. If you diminish that quality, you end up with a book that doesn't appeal strongly enough to either group to prompt a purchase. People buy products they want. Men will buy a book when it connects so strongly with their passions and interests that it moves them past their ignition temperature. No one buys a book, or any other product for that matter, because it "doesn't exclude them."

I hate mushrooms. I can't stand their texture, their appearance, or their flavor. Yet—and despite knowing full well they are a fungus—many of my friends and relatives love them. And what's more, they love them for the very same reasons I hate them. They love their texture, their appearance, and their flavor. If you removed the qualities that make a mushroom a mushroom, your attempts to pacify the haters would alienate mushroom lovers. Making a mushroom less "mushroomy" won't attract both groups.

Another mistake people often make is to covet demographic segments just because they are large. But a group's size doesn't make its members any more likely to buy. And, if they don't buy, it doesn't matter how many of them there are. These people are like logs. They may burn eventually, but it will take more than the heat from your marketing to set them ablaze. Instead, sell to the fuel you can light. Start your fire with the driest tinder.

TINDER

The driest tinder are the most valuable prospects for your product or service because they are most likely to buy, benefit from, and then enthusiastically promote it to targeted people in their sphere of influence.

For *The Purpose-Driven® Life* and the Forty Days of Purpose Campaign, the driest tinder was a group of twelve hundred pastors who subscribed to www.pastors.com, Rick Warren's Web site designed to serve ministers, attended Purpose-Driven®

Church conferences, read *The Purpose-Driven® Curch*, and used Rick's sermons and resources. For years Warren had provided them with research, sermon outlines, PowerPoint presentations, and other tools. Time and again he ran successful programs at his own church, then provided those programs to pastors. Those ministers were grateful, and they knew Rick Warren's materials worked because they had used them to create their own ministry programs. When he suggested those pastors take their churches through a multi-task spiritual emphasis he called Forty Days of Purpose, twelve hundred immediately agreed.

In October 2002, twelve hundred churches participated in the first campaign. It began with a video presentation of Rick Warren giving an overview of *The Purpose-Driven® Life* and how the campaign would unfold over the next forty days. For the next six Sundays, participating ministers preached sermons based on the book, using outlines provided by Rick Warren. Each of the four hundred thousand people attending those churches received the book and agreed to read one chapter each day for forty days. Those same people also formed groups of eight or ten and met in homes once a week to discuss the book's content and its implications for their life. Eager to share its impact, those people, in turn, bought the book as gifts for friends and relatives, they read it in public places, and they recommended it to friends. Within two months a small fire, one that began with a ministry program to just twelve hundred pastors, spread interest in *The Purpose-Driven® Life* beyond the walls of the church to produce a No. 1 bestseller with two million units sold. And that was only the beginning.

The Passion of the Christ nearly missed its driest tinder, and perhaps its amazing success. Most Hollywood films strike deals with major distributors who, among other things, design, fund, and execute the marketing plans for movies they represent.

Movie marketing budgets typically range from $20 to $40 million. Movie marketing plans target "moviegoers" and most often attempt to reach them through traditional mass marketing tactics. This approach assumes that people go to movies simply to be entertained and that they don't much care which film they see. It takes for granted that the movie with the most marketing will attract the largest audience.

The Passion of the Christ was different. One by one Hollywood's largest distributors, frightened by the film's controversial subject matter, refused to distribute it. Without a major distributor and its advertising budget, Mel Gibson was forced to fund the marketing himself. But he had just spent over $20 million to make the film and was reluctant to invest much more. Without a $40 million marketing war chest, Gibson couldn't afford traditional mass marketing tactics; he turned instead, and perhaps without realizing it, to PyroMarketing. The lack of a major distributor proved to be a blessing in disguise. The audience for *The Passion of the Christ* wasn't "moviegoers" at all. It was people who cared about Jesus. They didn't want to be entertained; they wanted their faith affirmed by cinematic art. A marketing plan aimed at the masses would have missed the mark, but without the money to reach millions, Mel Gibson was forced to concentrate on the handful of those most likely to buy.

Gibson focused on a collection of evangelical Christian pastors from across the country. He began by showing his movie to small groups of ministers, perhaps six to twelve at a time. As pastors spread the word to other pastors, the audience grew. Eventually Gibson showed it to rooms full of hundreds and even thousands of them. Those clergy, in turn, took their churches to see the film, rented entire movie theaters, and spent their own money to actively promote the movie to their community! The movie set box office records, but its marketing cost 95 percent less than most major films.

The Bible describes how Jesus launched his ministry in a similar way. Though he eventually spoke to crowds of five thousand, he began by directly calling just twelve disciples. These men were so inclined toward his message they responded after a single exposure, leaving their homes, their careers, and their possessions.

"As Jesus was walking beside the Sea of Galilee, he saw two brothers, Simon called Peter and his brother Andrew. They were casting a net into the lake, for they were fishermen. 'Come, follow me,' Jesus said, 'and I will make you fishers of men.' At once they left their nets and followed him."[2]

But just who are driest tinder and why is their ignition temperature lower than other people's? What makes them dry? Why are they always the point of origin?

SELECTIVE PERCEPTION

The human brain has been called "the best organized, most functional three pounds of matter in the known universe," yet the limits of its astounding processing power are tested daily by the deluge of data from our senses. Input to our senses of sight, sound, touch, taste, and smell easily exceeds the brain's ability to recognize, process, organize, and comprehend. Its limited capacity forces it to process information selectively.[3] It can't consider everything at once, so it chooses.

When presented with stimulus from both our eyes and our ears, for example, we prioritize that which is most relevant and attenuate the rest. In other words, "people create a world they can live in, and what they can't use, they often can't see."[4] While this process is nearly continuous, it isn't always evident because the brain seamlessly switches between various input sources as the data's relevance changes.

Not long ago I was working at my computer while waiting for a flight at Chicago's O'Hare Airport when I noticed the tail end of an announcement. ". . . Mr. Greg Stielstra, Gate G10." The airline had changed the gate for my flight and the public address announcer was giving the last call for missing passengers, including me! I made the flight, but as we taxied down the runway I reflected on what happened. Why did I only hear the last portion of the announcement? Why hadn't I noticed earlier broadcasts? The airline had, no doubt, announced the gate change. They probably said something like, "American Airlines announcing a gate change for flight 394 to Grand Rapids, now departing from gate G10." I realized that I hadn't heard the announcement, even though its sound waves had struck my ears, because the work on my computer was more important to me at the time. It was more personally relevant than "American Airlines" or "flight 394" or even "Grand Rapids." Those phrases could not break through my perceptual screen—the mental filter that allowed me to concentrate on my work by blocking the chatter of less relevant sensory input. It wasn't until the airline announced my name that my perception shifted. Suddenly the auditory information transmitted by the airport speakers was personally significant and at once my brain prioritized it ahead of the incumbent visual input from my computer screen.

An understanding of the human perception process is essential to PyroMarketing. Perception is the means by which people select, notice, take in, transform, store, and assign meaning to sensory data.[5] The process is the same for everyone, but individual results vary dramatically. That difference is the reason why ignition temperatures vary from person to person. Consequently, some will immediately notice your messages and buy your product after the slightest exposure to the heat from your marketing, while you could hold a blow torch to others without setting them alight.

STAGES OF PERCEPTION

As we process sensory information from the world around us, we progress through four stages: stimulation, registration, organization, and, finally, interpretation.

During stimulation, physical energy from the environment excites our senses transforming light, sounds, smells, tastes, and touch into electrical impulses that travel along our nervous system to the brain. However, stimulation can only occur once something is noticed, and to be noticed it must first be perceived. In other words, we can only perceive something we *already* perceive. This apparent paradox is, as we'll see, one important reason why the driest tinder are so susceptible to your marketing message while everyone else remains impossibly difficult to convince.

When sensory stimuli arrive at the brain, they undergo the second stage of perceptual processing called registration. During registration, electrical impulses are tested against existing knowledge to determine the level at which we should perceive the stimuli or, more important, whether we should process them at all. Prior to this, the perception process is external. That is, the physical properties of the stimuli determine our psychological experience. Until this point, the perception process is grounded in "facts." If a sound is louder, we perceive it as louder. When an ad is bright and colorful, we perceive it that way. But, with each stage in the perception process, the emphasis shifts. Beyond stimulation, personal traits begin to act upon sensory data controlling what we perceive. Objectivity is exchanged for subjectivity. Facts give way to interpretations. This new set of rules is why people say, "Perception is reality." Or, in the words of Friederich Nietzsche, "There really are no facts, only interpretations."[6]

Perceptions are formed by three influences: the physical characteristics of the stimulus, the relation of the stimulus to its surroundings, and the conditions within the individual.

Most mass marketing concerns itself with the first two of these influences and generally ignores the third. It seeks the consumer's attention by amplifying advertising's physical properties. Marketing becomes louder, brighter, and more colorful. Mass marketing also tries to control advertising's context by inserting ads where we least expect them. Targeting a captive audience, for example, is an attempt to control advertising's context.

The physical characteristics of an ad and its context are important but they account for only a quarter of the perceptual process. Louder, brighter ads may improve stimulation, but come no closer to being perceived. The old question, "If a tree falls in the woods and there is no one there to hear it, does it make any sound?" illustrates the problem. The falling tree generates physical energy, but no psychological experience. In the same way, an advertisement may generate sensory stimuli, but if no one is processing its information—if its message is irrelevant—it has no psychological impact. Louder ads remain silent. Brighter ads are invisible.

When I was young, my mom took a job with a company that brought Brazilian foreign exchange students to the United States. She would meet them at the airport and pair them with American host families. We stood at the gate the day the first group arrived. When they stepped from the Jetway, my mom tried to introduce herself. "Welcome to America. I am Judy Stielstra with SEA. I will introduce you to your host family." The Brazilians cocked their heads and shot each other quizzical looks. So my mom tried again. She stepped closer, waved her arms more vigorously, and nearly shouted, "Welcome to America. I am Judy Stielstra with SEA. I will introduce you to your host family." People around the airport turned to find the source of the commotion. The Brazilians stared. At this point I tapped her on the shoulder and whispered, "Uh, Mom. They're not deaf. They're Brazilian. They speak Portuguese."

The problem wasn't their hearing; it was a failure to understand. The perplexed foreign exchange students standing at the gate needed relevance not volume. It was their inability to understand English, a characteristic internal to the consumer, not the volume of my mom's announcement, an external characteristic that fouled their perception and prevented communication. This is why successful marketing must consider the conditions within each individual.

As people move through the stages of perception, "facts" gathered from their senses become less and less important as the significance of the meaning assigned by their mind increases. How do they perceive your ad? Is it relevant? What is their psychological experience? This portion of perceptual processing is internal to the consumer. Here an individual's mental structures, not the physical characteristics of the ad, have the greatest bearing on how they perceive it. Louder ads won't help. Stop shouting at the Brazilians.

INCLINATIONS

"We have mysterious inclinations," observed author Shirley Hazzard during her acceptance speech at the 2003 National Book Awards. "We have our own intuitions, our individuality toward what we want to read, and we developed that from childhood."[7] She was right, except that our individuality extends far beyond which books we read. We apply those unique intuitions to every decision we make—even the subconscious choice about which sensory stimuli to attend. These inclinations arise from an equally unique, but far less mysterious, physiology that also develops from childhood.

Although rare, infant cataracts are curable, provided a stricken child has corrective surgery within six months of birth. If they don't, then they will become permanently and irrevocably blind. An adult, however, can endure cataracts for years and surgery will restore perfect sight. The brain, not the eyes, reveals the reason. A typical brain has approximately one hundred billion neurons. Unlike other cells, brain cells have projections called axons and dendrites that reach out—sometimes as far as three feet—to other cells. A typical mature brain cell receives wires from about one thousand other cells and sends wires to about one thousand more, creating a complex interdependent network that makes the Internet look as simple as a child's connect-the-dots drawing.[8] Though the wires are laid, the connections are incomplete. Final wiring occurs during an activity stage. This stage is driven by experience and environment. Distinctions most of us make unconsciously at a glance—things like foreground versus background, moving versus stationary, vertical versus horizontal, and dozens more—are concepts the brain must learn. As the eyes receive this input and send it on to the brain, connections are completed.[9] Neural networks are built as neurons that fire together, wire together. If those connections are not repeatedly stimulated in the first few months of life, they atrophy and die. The brain wires itself through these neural networks and if we don't use them, we lose them.

We learn and remember through a similar process as concepts are stored, related to others, and reinforced. Our brains are teeming with a vast number of these interdependent neural networks through which we process all incoming information. These networks, and the information already stored in them, influence how and even *what* we can learn.[10] Musicians, for example, repeatedly exposed to the artifacts of their vocation, form and reinforce the appropriate connections and, in the process, becomes highly sensitized to musical things. Their nonmusical friend, by contrast, unable to relate the stimuli to prior experience, may not notice them at all. In a very literal sense, consumers are wired differently.

The more extensive a person's neural network, as it relates to your product or service, the lower their ignition temperature, and the easier it is to motivate purchase with your marketing. A person's ignition temperature is in an inverse relation to their interest, and their interest is the product of their life experiences and unique mental wiring.

This, in part, is why certain people are much more likely to buy your product or service, while others, missing the necessary neural networks, are effectively "blind" to your promotional messages. Some sensory data registers. Some does not. It all depends on each person's mysterious inclinations.

But even sensory data that passes the registration test is not assured a place in our mental repertoire. In fact, the brain doesn't store sensory data at all. Instead, it converts mountains of data into a smaller number of concepts. Concepts are abstractions— economical representations of larger amounts of data that enable us to function very efficiently. For example, if you had read *The Purpose-Driven® Life* and I asked you to explain its message you wouldn't recite it word for word. You couldn't. Instead you would explain the essence of its message, in your own words. You would explain its concepts. If I asked you to repeat that description, you probably couldn't do that either. Rather you would use new words to convey the very same meaning. You would reverse the perceptual process by converting concepts back into data—the spoken word.

Once we register a concept, the brain must store it. But where? Think of your brain as a filing cabinet. It has many drawers and within each drawer are many file folders. Everything is labeled and carefully organized. Your brain is a neat freak.

When the brain stores a new concept, it tries to place it into an existing file folder. It checks every drawer looking for a fit. When it finds a match, the information is immediately stored. When it doesn't, the brain must create a new folder, label it, and decide which drawer to place it in. This is the organization phase of perception.

Concepts that fit existing folders are easier to store and retrieve. Concepts that require new file folders are more difficult. Like a stranger at a cocktail party where everyone knows each other, unrelated concepts are wallflowers loitering at the periphery. It's difficult for them to join a discussion or get involved because they lack commonality with the other guests. But the brain is an excellent party host. It dutifully walks new concepts about the room, introducing them to others as it searches for connections, hoping to involve new concepts with the rest of the group. Therefore, the new concept is more likely to join an existing conversation than to interrupt the group with a new and different topic. Our need to classify things is so strong that, if something doesn't exactly fit into a known category, we will approximate to the nearest available class. In other words, we will actually distort new concepts so they better conform to existing classifications. This is because, to transfer information effectively, we must see the relevance of what we are learning and relevance is directly related to the number of preexisting concepts.[11] The more we already know about a topic, the easier it is to learn something related to it. Familiar subjects slide easily through the perception process because their path is lubricated by existing knowledge and experience.

The party analogy I just used doesn't only help explain my point; it also demonstrates it. By my connecting the unfamiliar concept of how the brain categorizes data with the familiar concept of a stranger at a party, you were better able to understand the new information. What's more, from this moment on your brain will use that association to retrieve that concept from memory. Cocktail parties and brain functioning are now linked in your brain.

Concepts, though important, are not enough by themselves. Humans crave meaning. Concepts without meaning are, well, meaningless. It is during the interpretation stage that meaning arises from the interrelationships among stored concepts. Meaning is the product of their interaction. Consequently, we can't understand concepts isolated from other concepts.

Memory also depends on meaning. The more connections there are to a single idea or concept, the greater is its meaning and the more likely it is to be remembered and easily recalled. In fact, without the web of associations among concepts it would be impossible to recall anything we had previously stored. Perception culminates in meaning. But for all its importance, meaning doesn't arise instantly. The transformation of data into concepts and their subsequent association takes time, a fact that Goldfish crackers and broccoli make clear.

What would happen if you let a fourteen-month-old toddler choose between a bowl of Goldfish crackers and a bowl of raw broccoli? Which would they prefer? Children choose the crackers, of course. But a psychology professor from Berkeley named Alison Gopnik and one of her students, Betty

Repacholi, wondered something more. How would children respond if they showed babies bowls filled with the two foods, then tasted each while saying, "Yuck" and making a disgusted face at one, and saying, "Yum" while making a happy face at the other, then pushed the two bowls toward the toddlers, held out their hand, and said, "Could you give me some?" What would the children do?

Not surprisingly, when the researchers liked the crackers, the toddlers gave them crackers. But when they despised the crackers and preferred the broccoli instead, the babies still gave them crackers![12] What was happening? The researchers realized that the children could not fathom someone liking something they didn't—especially broccoli. The idea that different people may have different, even conflicting interests and desires was a completely novel concept and one they hadn't considered despite plenty of supporting evidence. The babies had an abundance of data but hadn't grasped its significance. They thought that if they liked crackers, everyone must and they acted accordingly. In the same way, advertisements unrelated to a consumer's stored concepts are just meaningless data.

As the experiment was repeated over the course of another four months, the toddlers eventually caught on and began giving researchers whatever food they preferred, but it took time and repeated effort before this concept matured.

It's easy to see why Donald Broadbent, the father of human perception theory, insisted that a proper understanding of human information processing needs to take into account individual differences in personality and motivation. We dare not ignore people's mysterious inclinations because their mental wiring determines the meaning they assign to sensory data. When your product or service and its promotion fit people's interests and mental set, it is easy to get what *you* want. Your offer matches their desires and this inclination lowers their ignition point. Ask for a cracker and they will give you a cracker.

But if your product and its promotion are foreign to someone's existing conceptual set—if it loosely fits or conflicts with their interests and desires—then consumers will give you what *they* want. Ask for broccoli and you may still get crackers.

Attempts to convince, change, or persuade people are difficult, and time-consuming, and the outcome is uncertain. Don't try. While people may eventually change their position, just as large logs may eventually burn if held to the fire long enough, it won't be the heat from your marketing that does it. You only have one match and you must start a fire to survive. Use it on the driest tinder.

CAN YOU HEAR ME NOW?

Our brains actively engage in two kinds of perception, both of which influence advertising's effectiveness; they are perceptual vigilance and perceptual defense. Moment-to-moment perceptual vigilance, or "low-level perception," eliminates or attenuates sensory data depending on its relevance. Information related to our wants, needs, interests, and especially to the task at hand makes the cut and is passed along for processing, as with my gate announcement at O'Hare. Everything else is deemed unnecessary and is attenuated or rejected, like the dozens of airport announcements I never heard. Is it any wonder you can't remember the three thousand advertisements you saw yesterday? Perceptual vigilance spared you.

Low-level perception, for example, helps you safely drive

your car by filtering distractions that might interfere with the task at hand. The cocktail party effect is the best-known illustration. When you are talking with someone in a crowded room, it filters or attenuates other conversations so you can attend to just one.

Not long ago researchers gathered a group of Mexicans who had never been to the United States and a group of Americans who had never been to Mexico for an interesting experiment. They had built a binocular viewing machine capable of showing one image to the right eye and another to the left. One eye would see a traditionally American photo, a snapshot of a baseball game. The other was given a bullfight, a traditional Mexican image. During the test the pictures appeared simultaneously, forcing the subject to concentrate on one or the other. When asked what they had seen, American subjects reported seeing the baseball game while their Mexican counterparts had seen the bullfight. Perceptual vigilance, testing sensory input against existing categories and meaning, had selected the relevant image and suppressed the other. To which group would you rather promote a baseball game? Who, do you think, is the driest tinder for a bullfight?

Perceptual defense, or "high-level perception," is the other form. It is more complicated and even more interesting. Over the course of time we build up meanings. Those meanings become imbedded in our general stock of knowledge and eventually form a sort of background reality—the sum of our beliefs and attitudes—that serves as the reference against which we perceive everything else. That reality is the baseline for interpreting "facts." We are, therefore, self-referencing because the baseline against which we interpret facts is itself the product of our perceptual process and was once subject to the same interpretation. Consequently, in the words of essayist Anais Nin, "we don't see things as they are. We see things as *we* are."

What we perceive depends on what we expect. Perceptual defense amplifies, attenuates, or rejects sensory input depending upon how it fits a person's existing attitudes and beliefs. It molds incoming data to match our expectations thereby reinforcing existing beliefs while avoiding conflicting thoughts that might cause cognitive dissonance.

A classic study of college students demonstrated its effects. Participants were connected to a device that measured their level of anxiety, and then shown a series of words using a tachistoscope. Some words were neutral, while others were of a sexual nature and considered taboo. At first the words appeared so briefly it was impossible to recognize them. But each subsequent presentation left them on the screen a bit longer until subjects could correctly identify the words.

Researchers, measuring response times, discovered that participants took longer to recognize taboo words than neutral words. What's more, before subjects could correctly identify any word, they showed more anxiety over taboo words than neutral words. This suggests that our minds and bodies recognize and respond to visual stimuli before we become conscious of those stimuli and that sensory data that conflicts with our values and beliefs is processed more slowly, if at all.[13]

Twenty years ago researcher Stephen Grossberg introduced a model for understanding how the brain balances new sensory data with existing baseline facts. Grossberg wondered how, exactly, do we acquire new memories without displacing the ones we already have? Given the constant onslaught of new information, how do people remain who they are? He called his model adaptive resonance theory (ART). In the model all incoming sensory data were considered "bottom-up" signals.

"Top-down" signals, on the other hand, came from the brain and represented its learned expectations of what those bottom-up signal patterns should be, based on past experience. Grossberg suggested that top-down processing selectively amplified some features of a stimulus while suppressing others. This, he believed, helped focus human attention on information that matched our expectations. Neural networks in the brain, he reasoned, operated according to a specific set of rules. As a person entered each new situation in their life, their brain would begin to anticipate what might occur by remembering similar situations from past experience. To prepare for the anticipated events, top-down processing sensitized certain brain cells and suppressed others. He called this top-down priming.

To understand it, think of sensitized cells as having a value of +1, suppressed cells with a value of –1 and neutral cells— and those which were neither sensitized nor suppressed—as having a value of 0. If a neutral cell (0) received a bottom-up signal (+1), it could generate output (+1) and store a memory or initiate a response. If a sensitized cell (+1) received bottom-up data (+1), then it would generate an amplified output (+2) creating stronger memories and a greater chance of initiating a response. If a suppressed cell (-1) received bottom-up data (+1), the values would cancel. No output would result (0) and no memory or response would be created.

Perceptual defense places external sensory data at the mercy of internal signals. Consequently items, including advertising, that match our beliefs are amplified while those that don't are suppressed. Instead of becoming new and different people as we are exposed to sensory data, we continually become ever stronger, truer versions of who we already are.

Tobacco companies claim they discourage smoking by running antismoking ad campaigns. In reality, only nonsmokers pay attention to the antismoking message. The tobacco companies know that their customers, hooked on the product and averse to reminders of its health risks, will repress the negative message entirely. Big Tobacco, meanwhile, basks in the goodwill created by their apparent civic responsibility while knowing full well they have done nothing to harm their business.

An interesting side effect of perceptual defense is that who we can become is determined by who we already are. It really is hard for old dogs to learn new tricks. We become set in our ways because our ways are continually reinforced. Once a certain response is evoked by a stimulus, there is a great likelihood that the same stimulus will evoke the same response in the future.

Several years ago I celebrated Christmas at my in-laws' house. We were chatting in the living room while a video of the previous year's Christmas played on the television. During a lull in our conversation I made a joke in response to a comment on the video. A split second later I heard my videotaped self make the same joke. The stimulus had evoked an identical response from me two years in a row.

NEUROMARKETING

That some people have much stronger preferences for certain products, including those they have never before seen, is not just theory. Brain researchers are using new technology to sneak a peek at this process in action. The field of neuromarketing studies bloodflow, electromagnetic radiation, and other indicators that occur inside the brain when people experience strong emotions. Scientists use a functional magnetic resonance imaging, or fMRI, machine to monitor brain activity in real time. Subjects are shown a series of products and asked to rate them. Then they are placed in an fMRI machine and shown the pictures again. Whenever people see products they truly love, their brains show increased activity in the medial prefrontal cortex.[14] It's the hot spot. Activity in that area of the brain indicates a strong desire to buy. Unlike surveys where people can lie about their feelings, fMRI studies their intuitive response. When this portion of the brain activates, they want the product they saw and you've found the driest tinder.

FINDING HAY IN A NEEDLE STACK

Finding the driest tinder is easy when they are connected to an fMRI machine, but how do you locate them in the marketplace? *The Purpose-Driven® Life* allows us to contrast two approaches.

The twenty million people who bought *PDL* during the two years following its release were men and women, young and old, rich and poor. They were Hispanics, African Americans, Asians, and Caucasians from all fifty states and several foreign countries. They were waitresses and truck drivers, businesspeople and school teachers, politicians and professional athletes. And yet, for every young female elementary school teacher or retired African American insurance salesman who bought *PDL*, there were thousands fitting those same descriptions that didn't.

This presents a quandary for mass marketers because they tend to focus on demographics and *PDL* buyers were an eclectic mix that, on its face, didn't suggest any particular trend. Instead, it appeared that buyers were randomly distributed throughout society and could be nearly anyone (Figure 3.1).

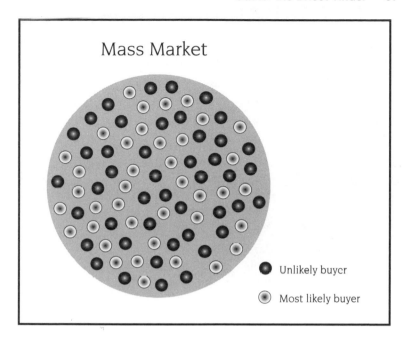

Figure 3.1 In the mass market the most likely buyers are mixed indiscriminately among unlikely buyers.

Trying to reach them with mass marketing meant that, while the campaign would find some of the driest tinder, it would waste most of its advertising on people unlikely to buy. Worse yet, the campaign would never reach most of those it could have influenced because it would miss more of the driest tinder than it hit (Figure 3.2).

Mass marketing response rates hover near 1 percent because, for any given product, only about 1 percent of the people reached by its message are the driest tinder. Mass marketers covet lower costs-per-thousand because they fixate on the wrong variable. Assuming they cannot change an anemic response rate, they try to reach more people.

With this approach, the most obvious way to increase

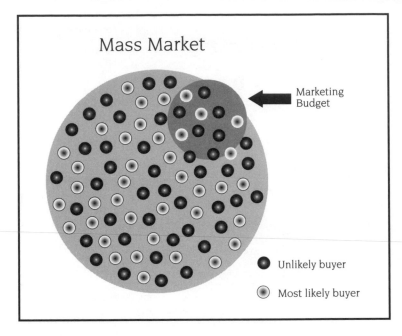

Figure 3.2 Mass advertising reaches many unlikely buyers and very few most likely buyers. You spend your entire budget long before reaching the entire market or even many of the hottest prospects.

sales is to increase advertising. To reach all of the driest tinder with mass marketing requires a budget-busting promotion, reaching hundreds of millions of people at an obscene cost and with grotesque waste (Figure 3.3).

But that's unrealistic. Most marketing people I know complain that their budgets are already too small. Companies cannot and will not fund marketing to this degree. And even if they did, why waste your budget this way? Your resources are limited. You get one match. Don't spend it on a method that requires an entire box.

"When your only tool is a hammer," said Abraham Maslow, "every job looks like a nail." To the mass marketer

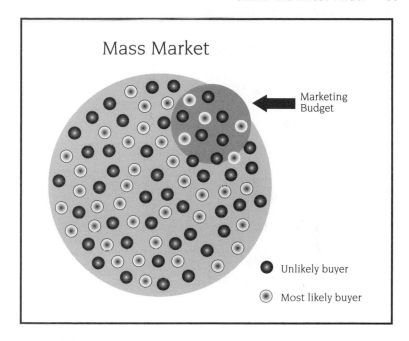

Figure 3.3 To reach all the most likely buyers with a mass marketing approach you must badly overspend your budget. No one has that many matches.

the driest tinder appear dispersed anonymously throughout society so their attempts to reach them involve tactics born of this assumption. But the same passions that lower their ignition point, making them easy for your marketing to ignite, are also behind another valuable characteristic—one that changes the game entirely. It's called homophilly. The term "homophilly" was coined by Kathleen Carley, professor of organizations and sociology, Carnegie Mellon University, and is a key assumption of her CONSTRUCT model of group behavior. It describes the tendency for people with greater common knowledge to interact. Or, put another way, birds of a feather really do flock together.

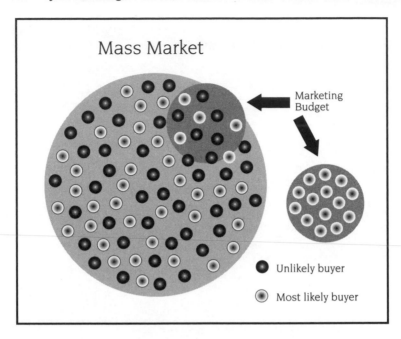

Figure 3.4 The driest tinder organize around their interests and voluntarily call themselves out of the crowd. By promoting to these groups you can reach many more of the most likely buyers without overspending your budget.

Homophilly calls consumers out of the crowd according to their passions. People organize around their interests and then build communications networks to support that organization (Figure 3.4). These organizations and their communications channels are the key to finding, engaging, and mobilizing the driest tinder. By making them the focus of your marketing it becomes possible to reach large numbers of the most likely buyers with your existing budget. Instead of promoting to more people, you promote to people who are more interested.

A focus on demographics couldn't reveal the driest tinder for *The Purpose-Driven® Life*, but a scrutiny of people's passions, interests, and behaviors quickly does. The first people to buy *The Purpose-Driven® Life* shared the Christian faith. Though their income, education, and ethnic heritage varied, they found commonality in their religious belief. Because these people cared deeply about God, they also cared deeply for a book that revealed his five purposes for their lives. And, while they were dispersed throughout the mass market most of the week, their religious devotion called them out of the mass market and organized them inside church sanctuaries each Sunday morning.

Green Bay Packers fans may look like any other citizen most days, but at certain times and in particular places they congregate with those who share their passion for the NFL's most storied franchise. Seventy-three thousand assemble at Lambeau Field for home games, regardless of the weather. Thousands place their name on the waiting list for season tickets. They come together in Internet chat rooms and on Web sites devoted to the green and gold. A Web site called www.southend-zone.com even lists Packers bars across the country including Moose Lodge 700 in Juneau, Alaska, an "America's Pack Official Pack Quarters Establishment," where you can gather on Sunday to share the game with other members of the Packers nation. Yes, people voluntarily call themselves out of the crowd, organize around their passions, and occasionally even wear foam replicas of cheese on their heads. Go, Pack, go!

Think for a moment about your product or service. Who are the people most likely to buy? What passion or interest has lowered their ignition temperature within the reach of your marketing?

I asked that question about a book I promoted for Zondervan called *The Case for a Creator* by Lee Strobel. Strobel, a former atheist with a legal degree from Yale and journalistic background that included a stint as the legal affairs reporter for the

Chicago Tribune, had written about the evidence from a variety of scientific disciplines that pointed toward an intelligent designer as the creator of the universe. Who, I wondered, would care deeply about that book? I realized that Christians teaching in public schools would have a special motivation. As a group they were prevented from teaching what they believed, forced to teach things they didn't believe, and routinely bullied in the teachers lounge by faculty that didn't share their view. Were this group to discover a book that supported their position with hard science, they would buy it in an instant. What's more, they would become unstoppable evangelists, spreading news of the book to everyone in their social sphere. They were my driest tinder, but how would I find them?

To identify the driest tinder not only did I have to know their occupation, but I also had to pair it with their religious beliefs. Fortunately, people call themselves out of the masses and organize around their affinities. Like gravity, homophilly was the invisible force that attracted them to each other. I quickly found an organization called Christian Educators Association International that organizes Christians teaching in public schools across the United States and around the world. CEAI forwarded my e-mail promotions to its members, offered me its mailing list, promoted the book at its convention, and volunteered to help in myriad other ways. They gave me instant access to the driest tinder.

Another organization called the Idea Center (www .ideacenter.org) specialized in starting student-led intelligent-design groups on high school and college campuses. They promoted *The Case for a Creator* to existing chapters, reviewed it on their Web site, linked to its Web site, and included its promotional materials in packets it sent new chapters.

By my focusing on the driest tinder, *The Case for a Creator* sold twice as many copies in the first six months as Zonder-van had hoped to sell in the first year!

Thinking about people's motivations leads you to the driest tinder and, just as often, to promotions you might never have thought of otherwise.

Suppose you are a Realtor representing starter homes in the suburbs. Who are the driest tinder? What about people living inside the city who have recently been burglarized? The day after a thief breaks into their apartment is the day they are most likely to buy that ranch home in the suburbs. Their circumstances triggered a desire to join a group called "Suburban Home Owners." They may even pay a premium!

Want to sell home security systems? Attend neighborhood watch meetings. That's where you'll find safety-conscious homeowners willing to buy your equipment and encourage others to do the same.

Selling full-size SUVs? Don't think about a prospect's income or age. Instead, try contacting people whose cars were recently rescued by tow trucks from a snowbank. Why not arrange with a local towing company to accompany them in a new four-wheel-drive vehicle on each run made by a tow truck and let the stranded motorist test-drive the SUV while their car is being extracted from a drift?

The driest tinder exist, no matter your product or service, and you can dramatically improve your marketing results by taking a few moments to consider their passions and where those passions cause them to congregate.

TURN OR BURN

You have reached a critical point in this book. It is here that you must decide whether to fully embrace PyroMarketing or return to traditional mass marketing approaches. Your answer depends on whether you accept the idea that successful marketing campaigns begin with a handful of the people most likely to buy and then grow, or whether your success depends, instead, on trying to convince millions of marginally interested prospects all at once. Will you advertise to those who amplify your message or those who suppress it?

Mass marketers believe that buyers are always a tiny subset of the people reached by their advertising. They don't really believe campaigns can grow apart from their advertising. They won't stake their success on the power of word of mouth. By this view it is impossible for a product's sales to eclipse the reach of its advertising. To sell ten thousand units they think they must advertise to one million prospects. To sell twenty thousand, they must reach two million, and so on. Consequently, mass marketers find advertising to the driest tinder limiting. They are afraid to promote their products to them exclusively because they worry there are too few to meet their sales goals. They are convinced their success is limited by the size of their match.

PyroMarketers, on the other hand, know they can only succeed by focusing on the driest tinder. The driest tinder are the point of origin, not the extent of the fire. PyroMarketers expand their impact by narrowing their focus to those most apt to respond. To sell ten thousand units of their product they need only reach five hundred of the people most likely to buy, convert them into evangelists, and equip them to convince their friends.

Whether you choose a mass marketing or PyroMarketing approach, the driest tinder are the only ones who will buy. They are the one group whose ignition point is low enough to be eclipsed by the heat from your marketing. The method you choose will not change who buys, only the efficiency with which you reach them.

The parable of the sower from the book of Matthew illustrates that Jesus understood PyroMarketing and the importance of the driest tinder or, as he called it, the "good soil." The Bible says a large crowd had gathered so Jesus climbed into a boat and told this story to the people assembled on the shore.

"A farmer went out to sow his seed. As he was scattering the seed, some fell along the path, and the birds came and ate it up. Some fell on rocky places, where it did not have much soil. It sprang up quickly, because the soil was shallow. But when the sun came up, the plants were scorched, and they withered because they had no root. Other seed fell among thorns, which grew up and choked the plants. Still other seed fell on good soil, where it produced a crop—a hundred, sixty or thirty times what was sown."[15] He finished by saying, "He who has ears, let him hear."[16]

When his disciples asked him why he spoke in parables and what this one meant, he answered, "The knowledge of the secrets of the kingdom of heaven has been given to you, but not to them. Whoever has will be given more, and he will have an abundance. Whoever does not have, even what he has will be taken from him. This is why I speak to them in parables." Though seeing, they do not see; though hearing, they do not hear or understand. "In them is fulfilled the prophecy of Isaiah: 'You will be ever hearing but never understanding; you will be ever seeing but never perceiving.'"

The size of the match doesn't determine the size of the fire. Ultimately, however, your success *is* determined by *where* you touch that match, regardless of its size. Every fire has a point of origin. What will be yours? If you foolishly chase after those least likely to buy, arrogantly believing you can convince them with your marketing, you will waste your match. If you greedily pursue the largest group, running from tree to tree with your match, you will burn only your thumb. But, if you begin with the driest tinder, patiently and methodically building your fire according to the irrefutable principles that govern both marketing and combustion, then there is no limit to what you can eventually accomplish.

CHAPTER SUMMARY

The driest tinder are the point of origin for every marketing campaign. Their life experience, passions, and interests regulate their perception process, which, in turn, determines whether your advertising will have any impact. It has been said that hunger is the best cook. Similarly, the quickest way

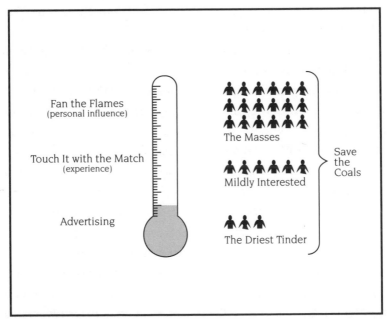

Figure 3.5 The heat from your advertising will only light the driest tinder. This is why they must be the point of origin. Everyone else's ignition temperature lies beyond its reach.

to improve your advertising is by targeting the most interested consumers. People who are either neutral or negative
remain beyond the reach of your advertising. But people
already inclined toward your product will actually amplify its
message, quickly moving past their ignition point to buy and
become evangelists for what you are selling. The driest tinder
are the *only ones* who will notice, remember, act upon, and
repeat your marketing message. Homophilly causes them to
organize around their common interests making them easy to
find and reach with your existing budgets. Only a fool would
market to anyone else.

FLASHPOINTS

1. Challenge assumptions. Why do your customers really buy
   your products? The people with a passion for *The Passion*
   weren't moviegoers at all; they were Christians interested in
   seeing the story of their faith told in film. Who are your best
   prospects really? What passion defines them? Why not ask
   them?

2. Dig deeper. Profile likely prospects and then look for subsets
   of that group that are even more passionate. Is the driest tinder for a dating book simply "singles" or even "single
   women"? What about single women whose friends recently
   set them up on a disastrous blind date? What about single
   women whose mothers called them every other day to ask if
   they had met anyone yet. Just when you think you've defined
   your market, go down a level or two farther to find the really
   dry tinder. You may not always be able to reach the groups
   you identify and very few traditional advertisers will have
   blazed a trail to their door. But, by applying some creativity,
   you can often find a way to talk with the most valuable

groups. What's more, the trail you blaze will be your own—often inaccessible to your competitors.

3. Identify where the driest tinder gather. The Gale Group offers an online directory of associations that makes it easy (www.galegroup.com). A quick search will reveal three pages of organizations devoted to knitting, or dozens committed to funeral homes. Learn how many members they have, when they meet, their Web address, and the other communications vehicles that support their organization by serving its members. No matter how seemingly obscure the interest, there are organizations that support it.

4. Search the Web looking for blogs, chat rooms, news groups, and Web sites devoted to the passions associated with your product or service. Start a dialogue with the people you find there. If you pledge to serve rather than sell, they will gladly tell you about the ways they gather with their like-minded friends and how you can tap into that network.

5. Past behavior is the greatest predictor of future behavior. The people most likely to buy your product are those who already have, so the first place to look for the driest tinder is among your existing customers. Locate them and begin touching them with the match and fanning the flames.

6. Take a moment to analyze your current advertising. Where is your emphasis? Is it on externals, or on the consumer's unique internal traits? Are you reaching the driest tinder or large piles of wet leaves?

Touch It with the Match

What one has not experienced, one will never
understand in print.
—Isadora Duncan

Touching it with the match involves giving people an experience with your product or service and its benefits. Traditional advertising can ignite the driest tinder, but it lacks the heat to set fire to all but the most interested consumers. Everyone else needs the additional power of experience. Testing and trying touches people in ways advertising can't. Experience, unlike even the most effective advertising, has the unique ability to capture people's attention, to excite their emotions, to enhance their memory, to promote their pleasure, to speak with credibility, to align with their expectations, and, in the end, to influence their preferences. *Experience heats marketing to new levels.*

An experience with a product's benefit quickly transforms prospects into customers. Without it, however, you cannot move people beyond their ignition point. Until you can build their interest to reach that critical temperature, you will be unable to build a fire, no matter how much fuel there is. In a market laden with prospects, but without sales, your business's potential will be fantastically impressive but will remain unrealized. Consider the illustration of the Minnesota Blowdown.

THE BLOWDOWN

On July 4, 1999, a cataclysmic storm walloped 477,000 acres of the Superior National Forest in northeastern Minnesota. Ninety-mile-per-hour winds struck the Boundary Waters Canoe Area Wilderness and cut a swath five to twelve miles wide by thirty miles long through densely wooded forests. The Blowdown, as it's called, split, broke, or uprooted twenty-five million trees. Many were twisted; their trunks snapped ten feet above the ground, before being strewn like pickup sticks across the landscape. Miraculously, and despite an increase in campers for the holiday, no one was injured.

Human lives were spared, but it was a holocaust for the trees. The dead or fallen timber, what's called "fuel load" for this type of forest, is typically 15 to 20 tons per acre. However, the U.S. Forest Service estimated that in the area affected by the storm that figure rose to between 50 and 100 tons per acre.[1]

The way the timber fell worsened the problem. Stacked as it was, air blew freely across every log. The wood dried quickly and completely, creating a glut of fuel so gigantic that computer models could not predict the behavior of a fire in the Blowdown.

Since 1999 campers have built hundreds of fires while exploring the Boundary Waters Canoe Area Wilderness. Countless lightning bolts from numerous thunderstorms have flashed across the sky. Heat from a relentless summer sun has baked the fallen timber. And yet, for all its mind-boggling potential, the

Blowdown remains unburned because it has never *experienced* fire. As with the felled trees of the Blowdown, it is not enough that prospective customers are aware of your marketing flame. There can be no fire until fuel is touched by the match.

FEEL THE FLOW

Even the physical properties of "catching fire" are instructive to marketers. According to the second law of thermodynamics, heat energy flows from warmer objects to colder objects until both reach the same temperature. This is why heat from a burning match transfers to other objects instead of staying in the match. The rate of heat transfer is driven by several factors including time, thermal conductivity, area, distance, and the difference in temperature between the two objects.[2]

We also know the relationship of distance to heat transfer is exponential.[3] That is, as you double the distance between an object and a heat source, you quarter the rate of transfer. Conversely, if you cut the distance in half, you multiply the heat transfer rate by a factor of four! This is why we must light birthday candles one at a time. The match will light the candle it's touching but, over even a short distance, its heat dissipates too quickly to light adjacent candles. If you are trying to start a fire with just one match, distance matters. You must close the distance between your marketing and the consumer's experience.

The closer we are, the more intensely we experience the power of fire. When the match is far away, our experience is minimal. We see only the light from its flame. Bringing it closer expands our involvement, and affects our senses in new and more powerful ways. The light from its flame is brighter, but now we also smell the smoke, we hear the sizzle, and, most important, we feel its heat. In the same way, experience closes the distance between prospects and your marketing message. Instead of merely exposing them to your advertising, you involve them in it. Promotion for your product or service becomes a holistic sense-stimulating event that conforms to the brain's natural learning processes in ways traditional advertising can't.

The Passion of the Christ and *The Purpose-Driven® Life* owe their success to this experience. Both used it brilliantly.

PASSION

Even after correctly targeting evangelical Christian pastors as the driest tinder for his film, Mel Gibson's success wasn't guaranteed. Though he had found an abundant source of fuel, he still had to touch it with the match. For all their interest in a film about Jesus pastors were still skeptical. This new film sounded good, but Hollywood had also given them *The Last Temptation of Christ*, a film that grotesquely distorted the biblical account of Jesus' life and ministry, and they were dubious about its ability to get the story right. Print ads in magazines popular with preachers might have made them aware of the film, but couldn't answer all of their questions. Direct mail brochures would not touch them emotionally or gain their support. Even movie trailers left too many questions unanswered. "They always choose the best highlights for those trailers," pastors would say. "What *didn't* they show us?" Nothing short of an actual experience with the film would convince pastors to watch it, or recommend it to others.

Mel Gibson touched pastors with the match by screening the entire film. He began slowly by showing the movie to six or seven pastors at a time, but soon expanded the tactic to include much larger events. More than five thousand pastors, representing all fifty states, saw the film at Saddleback Church in southern California. Five thousand more saw it at Willow Creek Community Church in suburban Chicago, and my wife and I were in the audience to witness its effect.

While waiting for the event to begin, the audience buzzed as pastors from across the country introduced themselves to their seatmates and swapped speculation regarding the film they were about to see. Cell phones were switched off, the lights were dimmed, and a hush fell over the audience as the film began. The quiet persisted throughout the film, punctuated periodically by the muffled sounds of crying as pastors who had committed their lives to the Christian faith were reminded of the sacrifice Jesus had made for them.

When it ended, the audience sat in stunned silence, still processing the deeply emotional experience. It was as if they had attended the Crucifixion. They more than understood the film. They knew it at an almost cellular level. Having seen it, they could recount each scene. With lumps in their throats they could testify to its power. In their minds they could clearly see precisely how the film would affect others. Their skepticism was gone. This was no *Last Temptation of Christ;* this was the story of Jesus they knew from the Bible and the one they had been trying to tell the people in their church for years. When Bill Hybels, the pastor of Willow Creek Community Church finally approached the microphone and broke the silence, he spoke for all five thousand when he turned to Mel Gibson and asked, "What do you need us to do?"

PURPOSE

Rick Warren understands the power of experience and designed it into his book and the campaign that spread its message.

A large number of Americans are aliterate and that figure is growing.[4] They are able to read, but they don't. Others start books, but rarely finish them. A book of more than three hundred pages, like *The Purpose-Driven® Life*, can seem a daunting task. Recognizing this, Rick Warren divided his book into forty short chapters and, on the very first page, spelled out a plan for reading it. He suggested reading just one chapter each day for forty days. By breaking his tome into manageable chunks he increased the likelihood people would read it. What's more, if they read it according to the plan he suggested in its first few pages, then nearly every reader's experience would be the same.

The book incorporated a number of features that involved the reader. Warren placed "Points to Ponder" in each chapter and encouraged people to reflect on them throughout their day. "Questions to Consider" led the reader to think about how to apply the message from each chapter to their life. Warren even suggested that people write their answers in the margin, further enhancing the reader's interactive experience with the book. Finally, Warren provided "Discussion Questions" and recommended that people gather with friends to read the book and talk about its implications. The product itself was designed to encourage and enhance the reader's experience. Unlike most authors, Rick Warren was not content with people simply buying his book. He wanted people to experience it because that was the only way they would be helped by its message and because he knew that, with the help of experience, disengaged readers become passionate evangelists.

As smartly as Warren designed the book itself, his Forty Days of Purpose Campaign became a breakthrough example of giving people an experience that permanently changed their connection to a product. Between October of 2002 and

November of 2004, more than nineteen thousand churches in the United States and around the world experienced the book during forty-day campaigns. The pastors in those churches preached sermons based on each of the book's six sections. Every member of the congregation committed to read a chapter each day from the book for forty days. Finally, those same people assembled into small groups of eight to ten in people's homes once each week to discuss what they had read.

By the campaign's end, every participant had been fully immersed in *The Purpose-Driven® Life*. They hadn't merely skimmed the book as they had so many others. They knew this one inside and out. They understood its message and were ready and able to share it with the world.

Traditional marketers recognize, but too often miss, the value of opinion leaders by asking them to do the wrong things. Had a mass marketer devised a church-based campaign for *The Purpose-Driven® Life*, they might have asked pastors to recommend the book during a sermon. They would have treated pastors like spokespersons and asked them to "pitch" the book to their congregation. They almost certainly would have failed. Rick Warren, on the other hand, focused on a ministry. He tried to serve, not sell. He never asked pastors to recommend his book; instead he gave them a turnkey program designed to help the people in their congregation improve their spiritual walk. He provided his $20 book to churches for just $7 so that everyone who wanted a copy could afford one. He offered the resources of Saddleback Church to ensure that every church enjoyed a successful campaign. He gave people a deep, meaningful forty-day *experience* with powerful content and the sales—more than 21 million of them in two years—naturally followed.

GIVE ME CHILLS

Wind chill is a popular but misunderstood concept used by meteorologists to explain how much cooler a breeze makes us feel. It is derived from the second law of thermodynamics, which provides that the rate at which heat flows from warm objects to cool surroundings depends on the temperature difference between the two. The greater the disparity, the faster heat will transfer. You become uncomfortable more quickly on colder days because your body loses heat to the surrounding air faster when the temperature is ten degrees Fahrenheit than when it is sixty degrees. But that rate soon changes.

As heat leaving your body warms the air around you, the temperature difference decreases. Instead of ten degrees, the temperature of the air next to your skin rises to twenty and, because the disparity is less, heat transfer slows. But, if that twenty-degree air is swept away by wind and replaced with more ten-degree air, then heat will again flow from your body at the faster rate. This continues until your body and the surrounding air reach the same temperature.

Wind chill describes the rate of heat transfer, not an actual temperature. A forty-degree day with a wind chill of twenty means that, because of the wind, your body will lose heat at a rate normally associated with twenty degrees. However, you will only lose heat until your body reaches the temperature of the surrounding air, which is forty degrees. Wind, no matter how strong, can never make things cooler than the actual air temperature. Water won't freeze on such a day, even with a twenty-degree wind chill, because the temperature never falls below forty degrees.

Traditional advertising is constrained by similar limits.

Additional ads don't increase marketing's temperature degree by degree without limit. Like wind chill, more advertising can't change its maximum temperature, but only how quickly that maximum is attained. If that maximum is below a person's ignition point, then additional advertising will not cause them to buy.

In fact, excessive ad message repetition can diminish advertisements. While a certain number of repetitions help cement the memory of an ad message, the human psychological traits of adaptation and habituation will undercut the impact of frequently repeated advertising. The brain adapts to repeated stimuli by decreasing its sensitivity to it. Adaptation, then, is a cognitive reduction in response to repeated stimulus. In other words, though our eyes and ears take them in, our brain stops paying attention to advertisements we encounter repeatedly.

Habituation is a physiologic response in which our sensory receptors actually stop firing in response to repeated stimulus. And so, repeated advertising cannot aggregate to a higher temperature because, as people stop paying attention to it, its impact reaches a plateau it cannot rise above. Interestingly, habituation is less pronounced when the stimulus has "special significance" to a person and so the driest tinder are somewhat immune to its effects.

But experiencing the flame is far more effective than reading about the flame. Through a single exposure it generates more marketing heat because, rather than battling against our natural processes, it matches the way we learn, remember, and respond. Our mind becomes an amplifier that increases a message's impact instead of a sentinel stopping it at the gate.

EXPERIENCE IMPROVES ATTENTION

When people engage in an experience, it becomes part of their daily thinking and behavior, as we interact with these new things and therefore understand them as part of the relevant world.[5] In other words, if you allow people to try your product or service in their natural habitat, you will gain their full attention.

I had seen countless television ads for the Gillette Mach III razor. Most involved men in towels shaving at sinks or stroking their chins as fighter jets broke the sound barrier and sultry women watched from the bathroom doorway. Gillette must have spent millions. Yet, despite these ads, I never felt even the slightest inclination to buy their razor. I already had a razor. It worked just fine. I already lived in the glide path for the airport and I was pretty sure my wife wouldn't approve of other women watching me shave. No sale.

But one day I received a package in the mail. A box the size of a VHS tape contained a free Mach III razor and coupons toward additional blades. The barrier to trial had been removed. The next morning I stood in my own towel at my own sink and shaved with the new razor. I loved it. I stroked my chin. My wife watched from the doorway. I bought a second razor for my gym bag and a third for my travel kit. I recommended it to my father and brother. And I just recommended it to you. What did that cost Gillette? They spent untold millions on television advertising that made no difference to me. I was aware of the Mach III razor, but so what? I hadn't purchased and until I did, Gillette had no fire. By comparison, it cost only about a dollar to give me an experience that resulted in multiple sales and free promotion in this book.

Television ads had little effect because the more Gillette ran the ads, the more habituation and adaptation desensitized me to them. I could remember the name of the razor, but I didn't care. As a passionate Green Bay Packers fan watching a football game, I didn't find shaving relevant to the task at hand. But by introducing a new product into my home, Gillette inserted it into my existing patterns—even into my hand—and enhanced my attention and my learning. But most important to Gillette, they made the sale. Ignition!

EXPERIENCE EXCITES EMOTIONS

Whether someone is overcome by the impulse to buy your product or service depends on his or her feelings toward it. Experience triggers our strongest emotions and emotions govern our behavior to an astounding extent. "All emotions are, in essence, impulses to act," wrote Daniel Goleman in his best-selling book, *Emotional Intelligence*. He called them "the instant plans for handling life."[6]

The word "emotion" comes from the Latin verb *emovere*, which means "to move," suggesting a strong connection between emotions and actions. That process affects the entire body, but, like so much else, it begins in the brain.

For all practical purposes, we have two brains: our logical brain, and the emotional one. The amygdala, two almond-shaped structures near the core of the brain, is our emotional center. It has more than a dozen distinct regions, each responsible for different emotions. The amygdala, along with the hippocampus, does most of the brain's learning and remembering. As the proprietor of fear and anger, the amygdala is vital to our safety. Impulsive and decisive, it is optimized to control our decision to fight or flee.

The neocortex is quite different. It is the thinking brain. It mulls information, processing it over and over, while considering the best response. It is rational, deliberate, and comparatively slow.

Research into neural pathways, the routes traveled by electrical signals in the brain, has revealed new insights into the relationship between the two brains and, by extension, a great deal about human behavior.

Sensory input from our eyes and ears goes first to the thalamus, where it is translated into the language of the brain. From the thalamus, signals travel over a neural network to the neocortex where the information and its implications are considered. Like a foreman at a construction site, the neocortex hands out work assignments. According to its chosen response, it distributes signals to various parts of the brain. When an emotional response is required, signals are sent to the amygdala. But the amygdala, like that friend who always gets the latest news before you, has another source. At the same time the thalamus is sending signals to the neocortex for processing, it sends a signal over another branch to the amygdala. The amygdala gets a sneak preview of sensory data and this shorter path enables an emotional response before the neocortex has had time to consider a rational reaction. "Those feelings that take the direct route through the amygdala include our most primitive and potent," says Goleman. "This circuit does much to explain the power of emotion to overwhelm rationality."[7] You have experienced the process if you have ever blurted out emotionally charged words that, given additional time to consider, you came to regret. The amygdala rushes in, leaving the neocortex the often-embarrassing job of cleaning up the mess. It also explains why counting to ten is an effective remedy for controlling one's emotions. Counting buys time for the neocortex to propose rational alternatives to emotional impulses.

Though we have two brains, they are not equal. A strong emotional reaction has the power to overrule a rational response. Consider cigarette smoking.

Between 80,000 and 100,000 children worldwide begin smoking each day, joining the ranks of the millions of adults who already smoke. About half of the people who begin smoking continue for another fifteen to twenty years.[8] Ask any smoker if their habit is harmful and they will reluctantly concede that it is and then, probably, light their next cigarette. You can remind them that every eight seconds someone dies from tobacco use, or that annually it kills about four million people, but it is unlikely you will change their behavior. Rational arguments or a litany of statistics make no difference. The smoker still smokes. Intellectually, people know the dangers and yet they continue. Why is it so difficult for their rational mind to overcome their addiction?

"Quitting smoking is easy," said Mark Twain. "I've done it a thousand times." The point he was making, of course, is that quitting is, in fact, quite difficult. Nicotine is why. Cigarette smoke is filled with nicotine that is absorbed quickly by the lungs and carried throughout the body by the bloodstream. Nicotine affects many parts of the body, producing an addiction that is both physical and psychological. Simply put, nicotine makes us feel good. As with positive emotions, the experience is pleasurable and we are programmed to repeat pleasurable experiences. That makes quitting very difficult, despite mountains of intellectual evidence.

Smoking cessation programs have dismal success rates. Only about 5 percent of people are able to quit smoking for even six months without medicine to help with the physical symptoms of withdrawal.[9] More often, though, smokers don't even try. Instead they smoke their way to the grave because intellectual arguments were no match for an emotionally charged addiction. Though people heard the reasons for quitting, they had *experienced* the pleasures of smoking and one was no match for the other.

But what if you fought fire with fire by exchanging intellectual arguments for an equally potent emotional experience? Are individuals more likely to change their attitudes on an issue when they actively participated in the persuasion process rather than passively listening to arguments? Can emotions, born of experience, succeed where logic fails?

In 1965 a pair of researchers named Janis and Mann devised a clever study to find out. They gathered a group of young women who were heavy smokers and invited them to imagine they were seeking medical attention for a bad cough. The women were asked to picture themselves at the doctor's office waiting for the results of X-ray tests. They were also asked to make believe that the researcher was actually the doctor treating their cough. Women, imagining themselves in this situation, spoke freely about their thoughts and concerns while waiting for the doctor's diagnosis and, as they did, their comments were recorded. At last the doctor shared the test results. X rays, he said, had revealed a malignant tumor in their right lung and they would need surgery immediately. The audiotape, still rolling, captured the women's response to this terrifying news.

Soon thereafter the researchers ran a second test. This time they played the recording of the first group's experience to a control group. These women were also heavy smokers but, unlike the first group, had not role-played the medical scenario. They had listened to a recording of the situation—a sort of testimonial advertisement for the dangers of smoking—but had no direct experience. The results affirmed the power of experience to elicit emotions and of those emotions to sway behavior. Subjects who role-played were significantly more likely than the control group to acquire negative attitudes toward smoking. But the experience changed more than their attitude; it also changed their behavior by reducing their daily cigarette consumption. Experience led them to cognitively rehearse the reasons smoking was bad for their health. Their mental rehearsal amplified the associated emotions and, in turn, equipped them to stop a behavior impervious to rational arguments.

While experience moves the match closer, most traditional advertising leaves people lukewarm. Very little of it can elicit emotional reactions as strong as those formed by experience because experience engages so many more senses and in much stronger ways. Experience stokes emotion and emotions move people to action. Emotions overrule our logical inclinations and even those habits formed by other emotions. "Making daily decisions based on emotions is not an exception," according to University of Iowa neurologist Antonio Damasio. "It's the rule."[10]

EXPERIENCE ENHANCES MEMORY

People remember experiences. In fact, experience is really all people can remember. The same process by which we experience reality moment to moment is responsible for storing that experience as memories. It makes sense, then, that if you want people to remember your product, it's best to let them experience it.

When we have an experience, we don't remember the

event. We retain the sight, smell, sound, and the associated emotions from the event in different parts of our brain.[11] But our memories, like meaning in the perception process, arise from the interrelationships among stored data. The relationships among those stored elements, what's called "patterning," is what constitutes our memory. It binds the disparate elements together, like pieces of a puzzle, which, once assembled, form a mental picture of events from our past. The greater the number of associated elements, and the more frequently they are reinforced, the more indelible the memory becomes. "Elaboration," as it's called, not only assures a memory's secure storage; it also contributes to our ability to access and recall stored data.

Experiencing drives elaboration. An experience with a product or service engages many more senses and in deeper ways than simple advertising. Think of the pastors watching *The Passion of the Christ*, listening to its sound track, feeling strong emotions, and comforting their friend with a pat on their shoulder. Or of the people who spent forty days with *The Purpose-Driven® Life* holding the book, reading and considering its words, answering its questions, discussing its content with their friends, and writing personal notes in its margins. The number of associations they made and reinforced ensured a deep and lasting memory of each product. Elaboration, made possible by experience, convinced them to buy, but it also equipped them for customer evangelism.

If you've ever forgotten something you once knew, then you realize that memory is more than simply storing data. A memory without recall is no different from a fact never learned. Interestingly, experience helps here too. Researchers have found that people can remember more when the demand for accessing stored information more closely matches the circumstances used to learn and elaborate it in the first place.[12] Memory relies on context. This places most advertising at a disadvantage because so few ads have anything in common with the situations in which the products they promote will eventually be used. If the people remember the product at all, it may be at the wrong moment. But if they learn through experience by testing a product or service in the very environment where they may eventually need it, then recall is enhanced.

Drinking Gatorade during a break from a three-on-three basketball tournament will enhance recall more than sampling it in a supermarket aisle. You are more likely to retain and recall a memory of a waterproof Columbia jacket if you wear one borrowed from a friend on a miserable day than if you see a magazine ad in the climate-controlled comfort of an airport. If you want people to remember your product or service in their time of need, then let them learn about it through an experience that closely approximates the way they will actually use it.

Memory and recall are influenced by elaboration but also by emotion. Experience stokes our emotions and emotions, in turn, imbue our memories with special significance. What are your most vivid memories? You can remember your first date, but probably not the second or third. You vividly recall your wedding day, but may forget your anniversary. You may know your exact location when President Kennedy was shot, or what you were doing when you first heard that terrorists had flown airplanes into the World Trade Center towers. But what, tell me, did you have for lunch yesterday? The difference between remembering events from your distant past in great detail and forgetting the contents of a meal you ate less than twenty-four hours ago is emotion and its influence on the human memory process.

EXPERIENCE MANAGES OUR MOTIVATIONS

Why people make the choices they do has puzzled philosophers, psychologists, and marketers for years. But a breakthrough discovery in 1954 began unraveling the mystery by shedding new light on reward mechanisms in the brain and their relationship to pleasure and motivation. When the rat race posed questions researchers James Olds and Peter Milner had trouble answering, they decided to look more closely at the rats.[13]

The scientists implanted electrodes into the brains of laboratory rats and trained the animals to activate them by pressing a lever. Each time they did, a small stimulation was administered to a specific area of the brain. It's called intracranial self-stimulation, and the rats loved it. Very soon they were pressing the lever over and over, repeatedly tickling their brains with tiny jolts of electricity until they were too exhausted to continue. The medial forebrain bundle was the magic spot. It's a communication pathway responsible for the brain's reward circuit.[14] Rats seemed to experience the most intense pleasure when electrodes were implanted in this particular area.

Training rats to press levers was nothing new. Previous experimenters taught rats to press levers to receive food or water. But in those tests the rats would act only when they were hungry or thirsty. This "pleasure lever" was different. The rats' actual biological needs didn't seem to matter. They would press the pleasure lever all the time.

As researchers probed deeper, they discovered that rats don't get to have all the fun. The same areas activate when people engage in pleasurable activities. Through further investigation, scientists discovered that a chemical mechanism, operating in these portions of the brain, was responsible.

Our brains are electrochemical devices. Electrical impulses trigger the release of chemicals called neurotransmitters, which, in turn, govern the behavior of electrical impulses. The chemical messenger dopamine is the pleasure drug. Its presence reinforces pleasurable behaviors. By blocking it scientists can reduce or eliminate an animal's pleasure-seeking drives. Without dopamine, hungry animals won't eat and thirsty animals won't drink. Rats with injuries depriving them of dopamine starve to death unless force-fed. Dopamine doesn't increase their appetite. Instead, a reward circuit in the brain, using dopamine as its messenger, made being hungry matter by associating pleasure with the process of satiating the need.

The reward circuit that we each possess influences our thoughts and guides our behaviors.[15] Its operation is summarized on bumper stickers and T-shirts that read, "If it feels good, do it." As we anticipate a good experience, our brains release a certain amount of dopamine. If our expectations are met, then elevated levels continue. If things turn out even better than we had hoped, dopamine is increased even further. If we are disappointed, then dopamine levels plummet. We learn by repeating those activities that feel good and avoiding those that don't.

Take eating for example. If our blood sugar level drops below a certain point, then the brain, responding to the sensation of hunger, makes us eat. Next, sensations of pleasure, triggered by dopamine, reward our actions. But, and this is important, it is the action itself and not simply its outcome, that we find rewarding. If we could pop a pill for dinner like the cartoon character George Jetson, it might restore our blood sugar levels, but it could not give as much pleasure as dining with friends. That's because the act of eating is what we find pleasurable, not the promise of food (advertising) or even the condition of being full.[16]

No wonder brands are built by positive experiences, not by advertising's hyperbolic promises. While the following was meant to define the human learning process, it more accurately describes how experience influences brand preferences.

> A behavior is a set of movements coordinated by the nervous system to preserve the structure of the organism. The basic behavior is therefore to approach or explore the resources available in the environment. When an action to acquire one of these resources is rewarded, this gratifying behavior is positively reinforced, and the strategy through which the need was satisfied is memorized.[17]

In other words, people search for things they need by sampling available choices. They prefer the one that works best and choose it repeatedly thereafter. That's brand preference.

If you want people to prefer your brand, allow them to experience your product. Not only will it increase sales, it can even improve your advertising's effectiveness. That's because, as learned behaviors are reinforced over time, dopamine release can actually transfer from primary rewards, like food, to reward-predicting stimuli, like seeing its packaging, or its promotion. As people come to associate pleasure with your product, they can begin to connect it with your product's advertising too, but there is no evidence to suggest it works the other way around. In a startling paradox, it turns out that while traditional advertising may not convince consumers to buy your products, experiencing your products may convince them to buy both your product and its advertising.

EXPERIENCE SPEAKS WITH CREDIBILITY

In business or in life, experience has no equal when it comes to credibility. We tend to trust what we have seen with our own eyes or touched with our own hands and that remains as true today as it was two thousand years ago.

The Bible says the disciple Thomas was not with the others when Jesus first appeared to them following his Resurrection. The next time the disciples saw Thomas they shared the amazing news that they had seen Jesus alive! But Thomas replied, "Unless I see the nail marks in his hands and put my finger where the nails were, and put my hand into his side, I will not believe it."

Consumers are skeptical too. They want to believe, but advertising's claims are often so outrageous and have disappointed them so many times that they demand a higher standard of proof. "I have a theory that the best ads come from personal experience," said ad man David Ogilvy. "Some of the good ones I have done have really come out of the real experience of my life, and somehow this has come over as true and valid and persuasive."[18] It may be more accurate to say, the best ads *are* experience. Advertising can never be as true and valid and persuasive as experience. Seeing really is believing. Seeing advertising often isn't.

The next time Jesus paid the disciples a visit Thomas was with them. They had gathered in a house and, though the doors were locked, Jesus came and stood among them, announcing his presence by saying, "Peace be with you!" Then he turned to Thomas and said, "Put your finger here; see my hands. Reach out your hand and put it into my side. Stop doubting and believe." Thomas said to him, "My Lord and my God!" Then Jesus told him, "Because you have seen me, you have believed; blessed are those who have not seen and yet have believed."[19]

Blessed indeed are those prospects who see only traditional advertising and believe. Most, however, like Thomas, need an experience.

EXPERIENCE ALIGNS EXPECTATIONS

All human evaluations depend on comparison. Thus, satisfaction is the difference between our expectations and our actual experience.[20] When a product we buy exceeds our expectations, we call it "good." When it fails to meet them, we are disappointed. Consequently, the way consumers feel about a product is a function of its promotion.

Products promoted with puffery and exaggeration will disappoint the people who buy them. When advertising over-promises, products underdeliver. Disappointing products can't recruit evangelists or feed the marketing fire because they lack Oh![2]. But, if the same product had been promoted honestly, through experience, consumers might have been quite satisfied.

A local restaurant in my town runs radio advertising claiming to serve "the best food in the world." While I like Brann's Steakhouse and Grille and eat there often, I would be sorely disappointed if I expected their sizzle steak to be the best cuisine ever to cross my lips. Brann's advertising set it up for failure by making a promise its products can't keep.

Experience, by contrast, aligns expectations with reality. It is what it is. With their expectations aligned, people are pleased, the product is remarkable (sufficient Oh![2]), and the fire grows.

The difference between satisfaction and disappointment is also the difference between a customer evangelist and a critic. I'm reluctant to recommend Brann's as "the best food in the world" because my experience can't support that claim.

If, however, Brann's had given me an experience, say, with a coupon for a meal, then my experience and Brann's promotion would align. Then I would tell my friends to try Brann's for a good steak at a reasonable price in a fun atmosphere.

EXPERIENCE REVEALS HIDDEN ATTRIBUTES

Diffusion of innovation studies how new products or fads propagate through society. Even if you aren't familiar with the concept, you have probably heard a few of its terms. Innovators, for example, are those people first to adopt an innovation. They are followed by the Early Adopters and eventually by the Early Majority. The Early Majority, as the name suggests, is a significantly larger group.

For years marketers assumed that Innovators, Early Adopters, and the Early Majority bought for the same reason. The Early Majority, they thought, simply needed more convincing. More advertising, they reasoned, would speed adoption by the larger, but more reluctant group. But more recent studies suggest something else.

While Innovators and Early Adopters buy a product for the reasons advertised by its manufacturer, the Early Majority often buys for other reasons entirely—reasons suggested to them by the Early Adopters but missing from the manufacturer's advertising. To use my Brann's example, Early Adopters may visit Branns hoping to taste the best food in the world but, based on their experience, recommend the restaurant to friends based on its value prices instead. In this process, Early Adopters perform a valuable service. They are translators, converting the restaurant's ineffective claim into something true and more persuasive.[21] Brann's food isn't the best in the world, but it is a very good value.

Marketers cannot skip quickly from Early Adopters to the Early Majority with traditional advertising because too often it communicates the wrong message. Experience, however, is true and enables each person to extract from it the most relevant and persuasive point.

EXPERIENCE INFLUENCES PREFERENCES

As experience holds our attention, excites our emotions, improves our memory, and heightens our pleasure, it eventually influences our preferences. We face myriad choices each day and as we do a portion of our subconscious brain quickly sifts through past experience for clues that will lead to the best choice—clues that only experience can provide and without which we would be lost. This is the lesson taught by the strange but true story of Phineas Gage.

In 1848, Phineas Gage was a twenty-five-year-old construction foreman managing a gang of men for the Rutland and Burlington Railroad as they laid new track across Vermont. Rather than twist and turn the track around the mountainous terrain, their plan was to blast straight, level paths through it. It remains difficult work today, but was doubly so in the mid–nineteenth century. The process involved drilling holes down into the rock and partly filling them with explosive powder and a fuse before adding a layer of sand and tamping the mixture tightly into the hole. An iron rod, about three feet long and about an inch and a quarter in diameter, was used for tamping.[22] It was placed into the hole and precisely pounded with a hammer. The sand is key because it shields the explosive from sparks that may occur during the tamping, but also because it forces the explosion down into the rock, rather than upward and out of the hole.

Tamping was Gage's job and he was masterful. But on this particular day he would make a tragic error. He placed explosive powder in the hole and asked his partner to add the sand, then turned and looked over his shoulder; responding to the call of another worker. An instant later he returned to his work, placed the iron bar down the hole and struck it with his hammer, but his partner had not yet added the sand! In a moment the iron bar grazed the surrounding rock and produced a spark that ignited the explosive powder.

Without sand, the explosion's energy blasted back out of the hole. Like gunpowder behind a bullet, the explosion propelled the metal bar out of the hole and through the head of Phineas Gage. It caught him in the left cheek, piercing his skull, and exited through the top of his head. The three-foot bar was traveling with such force and velocity that it passed cleanly through and landed more than one hundred feet away. Despite the horrific accident and to the relief and astonishment of his crew, Phineas Gage was alive! Within moments he was sitting up and even speaking. Gage rode into town on a cart, got off of the cart by himself, and conversed with the doctor who treated him. In the months that followed, he enjoyed a remarkable physical recovery. Though he was blind in his left eye, his right eye functioned normally. He could walk and talk and hear and carry on with barely a hint of the physical disability one might expect from such an injury, except for one thing. Gage was no longer Gage.

In his book *Descartes' Error*, Antonio Damasio describes the particulars of his recovery.

Phineas Gage will be pronounced cured in less than two months. Yet this astonishing outcome pales in comparison with the extraordinary turn that Gage's personality is about to undergo. Gage's disposition, his likes and dislikes, his dreams and aspirations are all to change. Gage's body may be alive and well, but there is a new spirit animating it.[23]

Prior to the accident, Phineas Gage was well liked. Smart, shrewd and polite, he was a hardworking man of unimpeachable character who maintained a keen ability to plan for his future while also looking out for others. He was, in short, a model citizen. After the accident, however, he became an animal.

His physician, Dr. John Harlow, said the "equilibrium or balance, so to speak, between his intellectual faculty and animal propensities" was gone. Harlow described Gage as

fitful, irreverent, indulging at times in the grossest profanity, which was not previously his custom, manifesting but little deference for his fellows, impatient of restraint or advice when it conflicts with his desires, at times pertinaciously obstinate, yet capricious and vacillating, devising many plans of future operation, which are no sooner arranged than they are abandoned. . . . A child in his intellectual capacity and manifestations, he has the animal passions of a strong man.[24]

Gage had forgotten more than his manners. He had lost the capacity to make good decisions. He was not merely indecisive or reluctant. Rather, he actively pursued the worst choices. It was as though he could not use knowledge gained from past experience to help with new decisions.

The bizarre circumstances of Gage's accident made his story both novel and popular at the time. That anyone could survive so massive a wound magnified its interest, especially with the medical community. But its most fascinating aspects would not become clear until years later as scientists deciphered Gage's personality shift and what it revealed about systems in the human brain. Phineas Gage, it turns out, was not the only one whose thinking was changed by his injury.

For years it was widely known that language, perceptions, and motor functions began in the brain. The new and amazing possibility suggested by Gage's story was that the brain might also contain systems devoted to reasoning and, in particular, to the personal and social dimensions of reasoning.[25] Those properties that make us human, such as the exercise of free will, or the ability to anticipate and plan for the future, or even the sense of responsibility toward ourselves and others, arise from certain parts of the brain and seem to exist independently of our intellect. This explains why Phineas Gage retained his mental powers, but not the ability to appropriately apply them, or, perhaps, why serial killers can be at once brilliant and deviant. But where do these systems reside and how do they function? It would be 148 years before someone would propose a reasonable answer.

Cartoon characters vexed by a difficult decision turn their head from side to side as a devil and an angel, perched on each shoulder, trade a repartee of contradictory suggestions. "Do it. You know you want to," says the devil. "You'll regret it for the rest of your life," the angel responds. "You know what's right. Do that instead." In real life, however, devils and angels do not stand on our shoulders, but, metaphorically speaking, it appears they may stand *between* them.

Antonio Damasio is the M. W. Allen Professor of Neurology at the University of Iowa College of Medicine and the author of somatic marker theory. He believes that people make decisions through the interplay of two processes. The first, like the devil on your left shoulder, is deliberate and goal oriented. It prefers immediate gratification and larger rewards and encourages both impatience and risk. "Do it. You know you want to."

The other, like the angel on your right shoulder, is a very fast, often subconscious, affect-driven process based on experience. During this process a person considers their options. They imagine the outcome of each choice and, as they do, the anticipated consequence elicits a visceral reaction based on previous experience: a gut feeling, if you will. A good reaction marks that choice positively and keeps it for consideration. "You know what's right. Do that." A bad reaction marks the choice negatively and rules it out. "You'll regret it for the rest of your life."

Our natural tendency is toward choices offering immediate gratification, no matter the risk. However, in normal, healthy individuals, the system intervenes when choices may entail substantial risks or penalties. The devil's impulsive suggestion is countered as the angel warns of its consequence. But what if there were no angel?

In 1994 one of Damasio's grad students, a gentleman named Antoine Bechara, designed a fascinating experiment to test decision-making performance. His results provide compelling evidence for the idea of somatic markers. He recruited two groups of people to play a gambling game. The first group had suffered injuries to the ventromedial portion of their brain, the same area Phineas Gage had damaged. The control group's participants were normal.

Bechara gave everyone $2,000 in play money, connected

them to a device that monitored their nervous system activity, and asked them to repeatedly draw cards from any of four decks. The decks were labeled A, B, C, and D. Every card paid the subject some amount of money, but certain cards also required the subject to pay money back. Decks C and D held mainly positive cards. Though their payout was modest, there was little risk of loss. Drawing from these "safe" decks meant the participant's winnings would steadily grow. Decks A and B, by contrast, contained cards with much higher rewards, but also many more cards with extremely negative values. In fact, repeatedly drawing from these "risky" decks would inevitably exhaust the player's money supply. Bechara told players the goal of the game was to maximize their winnings while minimizing losses.

Normal folks began by sampling all the decks and briefly demonstrated a preference for the riskier decks, but gradually, as they experience some losses, shifted their preference to the safer decks. They tended to stay with this strategy for the rest of the game. Normal subjects showed a nervous system response to winnings and losses. As the game progressed, however, they also registered nervous responses *prior* to choosing cards from the risky decks, but not the safe decks. Players grew nervous at the very thought of drawing a card from the risky deck. They had learned through previous experience that drawing from the risky decks often brought penalties. Somatic markings were warning them of the danger associated with that particular choice and they were learning to avoid it.

People with damage to their frontal brain, however, played the game quite differently. Like the normal players they began by sampling all of the decks but quickly shifted to the risky decks even though the penalties were so high that many players went bankrupt midway through the game! What's more, while both winnings and losses generated a nervous system response, brain-injured players never developed an *anticipatory* response. With no somatic markers, injured players were never discouraged from choosing the risky decks and repeatedly selected them to their eventual doom.

Our lives are filled with choices. Every consumer plays the gambling game as they stand in the supermarket aisle. Which product should they choose? "Take the first one and let's get out of here," says the devil. "No. Wait! We should carefully consider our options before choosing," comes the angel's reply. One by one the products are sorted. Product by product the mind quickly, and subconsciously, imagines the consequence of each selection. Logic circuits activate and past experience, labeled with somatic markers, is summoned. The very existence of somatic markers, in turn, depends on prior experience. Will consumers recall an experience with your product?

New products are unknown and a risk. "Avoid it," says the angel. Products promoted with outlandish promises made through traditional advertising probably disappointed. A negative somatic marker alerts the consumer and the angel warns, "They lied to us before, better not trust them." But, if you touched consumers with the match, if you gave them an experience with your product or service, then they have an honest appreciation of its benefits and a positive somatic marker. "That's the one we tried and loved before. Let's get it again," says the angel as the consumer places your product into their cart.

GRAY MATTERS

Brain-based learning is a popular trend in education. It argues, quite sensibly, that children will learn more easily if teaching methods conform to their brain's natural processes. It's an idea that makes so much sense it makes you wonder why no one thought of it before. Traditional schooling, on the other hand, like so much traditional advertising inhibits learning by discouraging, ignoring, or punishing the brain's innate procedures. After decades of trying to beat the brain, many smart teachers have decided to join it.

Knowing what they do about the natural learning process, brain based educators hold to several core principles. First, they are conscious that the brain is a parallel processor, capable of performing many activities at once. They also acknowledge that natural learning engages the whole physiology. The more our senses are involved, the more our mind will be too. They recognize that the search for meaning is innate and comes through patterning—the relationship among stored concepts in the brain—which, in turn, depends on experience.

Brain-based educators recognized that your brain had a method for acquiring knowledge long before schoolteachers and marketers devised methods for teaching and promoting. It came with an instinctive process for understanding the world, drawing conclusions about it, and responding appropriately. The learning method your brain has been using for years and still prefers is experience. Not only is experience the best teacher; it is the best marketer as well. When you touch people with the match, you heat marketing to new levels, igniting many more people along the way.

If you've gathered the driest tinder and touched it with the match, then your marketing fire is burning brightly, but even more can be accomplished once you learn to fan the flames.

CHAPTER SUMMARY

Touching people with the match means giving them an experience of your product or service. By experiencing its benefit through all their senses, you activate existing patterns and attract the consumer's attention. Experience unlocks the persuasive power of emotions and prints memories in bold type. Experience, not advertising, triggers the human reward circuit. Rein-

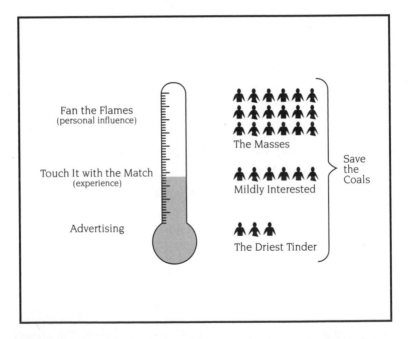

Figure 4.1 Experience generates more heat than typical advertising and has the power to reach that larger segment of prospects who are mildly interested. Experience helps you increase the heat and your reach.

forced by dopamine, it allows people to feel the pleasure of satisfying their need and conditions them to choose it again and again. Experience alone creates the somatic markers that enable consumers to choose your product from myriad options. Experience touches the driest tinder with the match.

FLASHPOINTS

1. Does your current marketing give people an experience with your product or service? Are you trying to make people laugh by telling them you're funny or by telling them a joke?
2. Where do people naturally use your product or service? How can you enable them to try it under those same circumstances?
3. Can you test the power of experience to enhance memory? Give one group of prospects an experience and expose another to your advertising before testing them both on their ability to recall salient facts. Which group remembers better?
4. Does your advertising match the consumer's actual experience with your product? Or does your advertising foster disappointment by overpromising? Make sure a consumer's experience with your product exceeds the expectations created by its advertising. That's a formula for satisfied customers.
5. What do customers love about your product? Are the real benefits the same as the ones you advertise, or have your customers identified a hidden benefit that would actually help you sell more? Find out what your customers love about your product or service and feature it in your advertising.

Fan the Flames

You can blow out a candle, but you can't blow out a fire.
Once the flames begin to catch, the wind will blow it higher.
—Peter Gabriel, *Biko*, 1980

There was perhaps no better, or more entertaining, study of human behavior than the old television program *Candid Camera*. The show's creator, Allen Funt, said it was about "catching people in the act of being themselves," and he devised goofy traps that allowed for this week after week.[1] Beyond entertaining, these stunts often highlighted truths about human behavior better than situational experiments fashioned by social psychologists. An episode called "Face the Rear" stands out and illustrates the implausible power of personal influence.

In "Face the Rear," an unsuspecting "victim" boarded an elevator and turned around to face the doors, just as most people would. However, the next three people to get on—*Candid Camera* actors—faced the rear. The camera captured the victim's uncertainty. Why were these people facing the rear? Did they know something he didn't? What should he do?

When the fourth person stepped onto the elevator and also

faced the rear, the pressure became unbearable and, as the elevator doors closed, the victim could be seen turning, though he did not quite know why, to join the other riders by facing the rear.

HOT, HOT, HOT!

The reason, of course, is that he bowed to the influence of his fellow riders, something most people do, metaphorically speaking, each time they buy something. One research firm reports that 92 percent of consumers made a purchase decision in the last year based on someone else's opinion.[2] Another survey found that word of mouth is a growing influence, with 38 percent of Americans calling it "extremely" or "very" influential in buying decisions. More people buy religious books because of a personal recommendation than any other reason. It is dramatically more influential than cover art, price, reviews, displays, advertisements, publicity, bestsellers lists, or endorsements. In fact, by itself personal recommendation prompts purchase more effectively than advertising, publicity, endorsements, bestseller lists, and seeing the author in person *combined!*[3]

The bottom line is this: people spread messages more effectively than advertising. The fire is hotter than the match. This is why the process that spreads your marketing message must be different than the one by which it began.

The coal fires in a blacksmith's forge burn at between 500 degrees and 900 degrees Fahrenheit. That is, until they crank the bellows. By cranking the bellows, the blacksmith fans the flames, feeding air to the fire, enhancing the reaction and rapidly raising the fire's temperature to 2,500 degrees or more. If it were possible to supply pure oxygen, then the coal would burn at an astounding 3,590 degrees Fahrenheit[4]—seven times hotter than the original fire and nearly one-third the temperature of the sun's surface![5]

Fanning the flames increases a fire's temperature, allowing it to light fuels with higher ignition points. Fuels beyond the reach of the original fire cannot resist the higher temperatures of one that's been fanned. In PyroMarketing, fanning the flames involves equipping your customers to spread your message through word of mouth. Word of mouth isn't what happens in the absence of marketing; it's the natural consequence of marketing done right. It is the force behind the incredible success of *The Passion of the Christ* and *The Purpose-Driven® Life,* or any other runaway movement. It is how ideas, messages, behaviors, and trends spread. Harnessing its power is the key to expanding a fire beyond its point of origin.

It is not enough anymore simply to find buyers for your product or service. Converting them into zealous evangelists and equipping them to influence others is what you must do next.

Mass marketers were taught that marketing involves a single step—that it's something businesses do *to* consumers. But this approach values people only for their "purchase potential" and ignores their "promotional potential." It favors prospects over customers, and it wrongly assumes mere advertising can convince anyone. Once you get beyond the driest tinder, however, people's ignition temperatures soar and advertising alone—or even experience—may not convert them.

PyroMarketing takes a different view. Making the initial sale is an important first step to building a marketing fire, but accounts for only half the process. You must also equip those same customers to effectively spread your marketing message. It's something they are naturally inclined to do and if you have placed something beneficial into the hands of grateful customers, if you have gathered the driest tinder, touched it with the match and made the sale, then by fanning the flames you can transform those initial buyers into customer evangelists whose personal influence makes an unstoppable marketing force.

Before you can harness the power of personal influence, you must first understand the various ways it works.

SOCIAL PROOF

A staggering array of personal differences distinguishes the six billion people walking our planet. Trying to understand their individual behavior can be confounding enough; you'd think that to also consider how groups of them interact would complicate things to a bewildering degree. But that isn't always the case. An individual's behavior can be mysterious indeed, as the parent of any teenager will attest. But while some social interaction defies prediction, other kinds are surprisingly knowable. The manner in which people interact is of vital importance to marketers because human social connection and communication are at the core of cultural phenomena like *The Purpose-Driven® Life* and *The Passion of the Christ* and how they propagate through customer populations. Those influences take many forms. Let's begin by looking at one called social proof.

Walter Lippmann, the great American journalist and social philosopher, said, "Where all think alike, no one thinks very much," and social psychologist Solomon Asch proved it.[6] In the 1950s, Asch conducted a series of fascinating experiments in which he presented a slide show to groups of eight people. Each slide contained vertical line segments of varying lengths similar to the example below.

One by one, subjects were asked which of the three lines on the right was the closest in length to the line on the left. It seems like a simple test since the answer is clearly "C." Complicating matters, however, was the fact that only one member of the group was actually a subject. The other seven were plants with instructions to give an incorrect answer, such as "A." This pro-

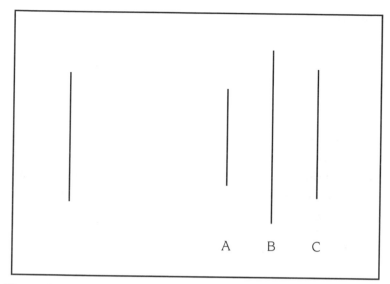

Figure 5.1 Example of slide used by Solomon Asch.

duced a terrible conflict. The subjects knew "C" was correct but as the others repeatedly chose "A" they became less certain of their own judgment. In fully one-third of the cases the subjects ignored the evidence seen with their own eyes and agreed instead with the unanimous, but incorrect, opinion of the group.

In a purely rational world other people's choices shouldn't affect our own. Knowing that each choice carried a different consequence, people should choose the alternative with the greatest benefit, based on their personal tastes and knowledge of the options. It's what economists call the transaction. Within the transaction, a person's self-interest should determine which book to read or which movie to see, or even which line segment they found similar to another. What's more, people with the same preferences should make all the same choices. In such a world other people's opinions wouldn't matter because, so long as their preferences were the same, their choices would also match.

This scenario, however, is upset by the messy complexities of human behavior. For starters, people have very different preferences. From mushrooms to football teams, what one person loves, another may hate. Nevertheless, each individual should still choose according to his or her personal preference.

The trouble is that many problems are too complicated to accurately assess. People know their preferences, but not nearly enough about their options and this leaves them uncertain and unable to decide. As product choices increase, so does their dilemma. "Americans today choose among more options in more parts of life than has ever been possible before," observed sociologist Barry Schwartz in an article he wrote for *Scientific American* called "The Tyranny of Choice."[7] The avalanche of information made possible by the Internet and the constant barrage of advertising confuse things even further. Today, it's difficult to even know all the options let alone evaluate them. The number of products and the availability of information about them is constantly increasing, but our mental capacity has remained virtually unchanged. Choosing a phone company was easy when advertisements on three television networks promoted a single choice. Trying to figure out the best wireless provider from the confusing array of companies, plans, and options, though, is nearly impossible.

Whether our uncertainty about which option to choose comes from a lack of information or more information than we can process doesn't matter. Either way, these limitations prevent us from making an independent, rational choice because of a condition social scientist Herbert Simon called bounded rationality.[8] Here limits on information and cognition constrain our ability to choose intelligently. Uncertain and unable to figure it out on our own, we reach beyond the transaction—past our internal preferences and knowledge of alternatives—to what economists call decision externalities.[9] As if cheating on a test, we stop trying to solve the problem ourselves and begin looking at our neighbor's answer. From which new book to buy to which direction to face on the elevator, psychology professor Robert Cialdini says, "we view a behavior as more correct in a given situation to the degree that we see others performing it."[10] Psychologists call it social proof.

"Of one hundred men," said evangelist Dwight L. Moody, "one will read the Bible; the ninety-nine will read the Christian."[11] By one definition, the driest tinder are those prospects who decide to buy your product or service without the help of externalities. They are the one who reads the Bible. Their greater expertise and interest allow them to make the best choice without help from an outside influence. For example, I am an audiophile and have been since I was young. I have worked in a stereo shop, a recording studio, several radio stations, and as a sound reinforcement engineer. I even design and build my own loudspeakers. Understandably, I often buy a new piece of electronics without consulting anyone. My history, experience, knowledge, and interest enable me to choose for myself. Many of my friends, on the other hand, love music and want a great stereo but don't know a woofer from a tweeter. They are ill equipped to make their own decision and routinely talk with me before entering a store. They are the ninety-nine who read the Christian. Not surprisingly, my recommendation strongly influences their choice.

This is an important reason why the driest tinder are always the point of origin. Trends must begin with them because only the driest tinder can decide to buy without waiting for another person's influence. To varying degrees, everyone else requires externalities and must delay their own selection until the people whose opinions they follow have made their choice. Thus every market is divided into initiators and imitators. The driest tinder are initiators because they act first. Their ignition point is low and the slightest heat from your marketing sets them alight. Everyone else is an imitator. Their uncertainty increases their ignition temperature, and so they must wait for the heat of personal influence—for other people to establish the "appropriate behavior" before they can copy it.

Uncertainty can exist after a purchase as well. It's called buyer's remorse and it describes the dissonance we sometimes feel after plunking down our money for some new gadget. Surprisingly, buyer's remorse can actually contribute to positive word of mouth. Here again social proof soothes our anxiety because, like radiative feedback in a fire, it works in both directions. Not only do we look to other people when making decisions, we often rely on others to confirm those choices we have already made. That is why, when people buy a new product or service, they recommend it to their friends and family. The more people we convince to buy the same item, the more confident we are that our choice was correct. "I must have bought the best brand," we think, "look at all the others who followed my lead."

TRANSITIONS

When some of the driest tinder have purchased but many other prospects have yet to buy, the marketing process reaches a critical point. This is where the forces that started the fire give way to the ones that will cause it to spread. The fire moves from the incipient phase to the steady-state burning phase by leaping from the tinder where it began to surrounding fuel.

From this point forward the fire's growth will depend on

the heat released by the fire itself. The driest tinder have already purchased your product, experienced, and are actively recommending it to friends in hopes of further confirming their choice. Customer prospects, with their higher ignition temperature and greater uncertainty are looking for the social proof that will help them make a choice. Customer evangelists are recommending and releasing their greatest heat just as prospects in need of advice draw near to receive it.

The less we know about a choice, the greater our uncertainty and the more we rely on others. Social proof, as a result, becomes increasingly important as a person's ignition temperature rises and their attention shifts from your marketing to the people around them. Not all influences are equal, however. Certain peo ple, relationships, and circumstances exert a disproportionate influence over our choices.[12] By understanding those differences, you can design marketing programs that take advantage of them and better fan the flames of your growing fire.

PAYING ATTENTION

Nature may abhor a vacuum but it loves synchrony. Synchrony occurs when independent entities such as a nation of moviegoers, or twenty million book buyers, or people applauding at a concert begin to act in unison. The splatter of ten thousand clapping hands suddenly finds its rhythm and hammers out a single beat. In Southwest Asia millions of fire flies assemble in mangrove trees, their tails blinking randomly like twinkling Christmas lights. Then, a few moments later, they synchronize turning the tree into a pulsing strobe light.[13] It's called self-organization because no one leader coordinates the group's actions. Synchrony emerges instead from the interplay of the group's individual members in a way that scientists are only now beginning to understand. Runners on a track illustrate the forces involved.

Have you ever noticed how despite differences in individual talent, speed, and stamina, Olympic runners cluster together? Their differing abilities should have dispersed them around the track in an "asynchronous state" as faster runners separated from and later lapped the slower athletes, but that isn't what happens at all. In a race there exist competing pressures. Every runner wants to remain within striking distance of the leader, just as the leader fears burning out by running ahead of the group. In this situation the runners not only monitor their own speed and endurance, but more important, they pay careful attention to the runners around them. If their abilities vary too widely, synchronization isn't possible. A group of elementary school children, for example, cannot stay with world-class adult athletes. However, provided the runners are reasonably alike and also motivated, synchrony will result. Despite similar abilities, Sunday joggers, by contrast, are often oblivious to other runners and can be scattered almost anywhere on a track or throughout a park because they lack comparable incentives.

Paying attention to others enables synchrony and, in the words of sociologist Duncan Watts, "We humans continuously, naturally, inevitably, and often unconsciously pay attention to each other when making all manner of decisions, from the trivial to the life changing."[14] Every day our thoughts, feelings, and behaviors are influenced by the actual, imagined, or implied presence of others. Paying attention is simply how the process begins.

WATCH AND LEARN

Personal experience may be the best teacher, but it is not the only one. We can also learn by observing other people's personal experience. Allowing prospects to try your product quickly raises their temperature beyond the ignition point, but it also spreads the fire by radiating heat to those around them.

In the late 1960s and early 1970s psychologist Albert Bandura conducted a series of studies designed to cure children of their fear of dogs. He showed them short videos of children encountering dogs. Sometimes the children were alone; other times they were part of a group, but in every case the child who encountered the dog displayed no fear and would move closer and closer until he or she could pet the animal and later feed it.

A month later the same children were placed in a situation where they had to directly interact with an unfamiliar dog—a circumstance that would have terrified them previously. Those who had seen the video of individual children with a dog were able to approach the dog with a new confidence. Those who had seen video of groups of children interacting with dogs were better still.

This and other experiments led Bandura to postulate that, in addition to learning through their own experience, people also learn by watching others and adjust their behavior by vicariously experiencing the positive or negative consequences of someone else's choice. After watching the mechanical bull dislocate your buddy's shoulder, for example, you may decide to drop your money into the jukebox instead. But if your friend rides it easily, and adoring fans promptly surround him, you might press your way to the front of the line.

Through a series of experiments Bandura discovered the principles undergirding his "social learning theory." First, he noticed that people are more likely to imitate someone they like. Mimicry increases when the observer finds the example setter to be smart, attractive, or popular. Just how much the observer copies them depends to a great degree on how much they want to be like them. This makes a person's circle of friends and family especially influential.

But, perhaps more important, whether an observer copies modeled behavior also depends on how much they believe they *are already like them*. People follow others' examples because they want the same outcome. But if that outcome depends on skills they don't possess—if the example setter is different— then they worry that the outcome may be different too and are less likely to follow their lead. When people believe they are like the example setter, however, the power of observational learning to influence behavior jumps dramatically. The same research study that found personal recommendation most influences book purchases also found that its influence more than doubles when the recommendation occurs in a church setting. Where similar people share a common bond, both liking and likeness increase and amplify the power of observational learning. Not only do we learn from those who are like us, we actually learn to be more like other people.

SWEET EMOTIONS

"Wayne's World," the comedy sketch starring Mike Myers and Dana Carvey as cohosts of a goofy cable access television show, began on *Saturday Night Live* in the early 1990s before spawning a movie and catch phrases like "Party on" and "Schwing!" Along the way it hinted at a fascinating curiosity of human social behavior with seismic implications for marketing.

In one episode, Garth's cousin Barry (played by Tom Hanks) is a roadie for Aerosmith and convinces the band to appear on the show to promote an upcoming concert. When the band joins them on the set, Garth convulses and blurts out, "Wayne, I'm so excited, I think I'm going to hurl."

Wayne, who had been feeling fine until Garth's announcement, warns, "Garth, get it together, man, don't hurl, 'cause if you hurl and I catch a whiff of it, man, I'm gonna spew. And if I blow chunks, chances are someone else is going to honk, alright? And that's going to set off a peristaltic chain reaction."

Could Garth somehow give his anxiety to others? Garth's tummy was turning somersaults from the joy—or stark terror—of meeting his favorite band. Was it possible for Wayne to "go totally mental" and catch Garth's emotions? And could those emotions and their physical effects spread quickly throughout an entire group? The surprising answer is yes.

A sizeable collection of science dating back decades supports the idea that people tend to "catch" each other's emotions, moment to moment. The authors of the book *Emotional Contagion* contend: "When people are in a certain mood, whether elation or depression, that mood is often communicated to others. Talking to a depressed person we may feel depressed, whereas talking to someone who feels self-confident and buoyant, we are likely to feel good about ourselves."[15]

The contagious nature is not limited to a select few emotions, but applies to the full range of human feelings. Many people find this news difficult to believe because they can't readily remember it happening to them. But that's because the process by which it operates is so subtle. Our mental states are not limited only to conscious and unconscious. There is a third that occupies a middle ground. It is here that emotional processing resides, often inaccessible to our conversant awareness, helping us to imperceptibly monitor and synchronize with the other runners on our social track.[16]

Emotional contagion may help explain why personal recommendations are so much more powerful than other forms of promotion. If someone feels good about a product they rec-

ommend, we are likely to catch their good feelings as they recommend it. What's more, we may come to associate those
good feelings directly with the recommended product and we
are much more likely to buy products that make us feel good.
But how does it happen? How can we "catch" someone else's
emotions? It occurs in a way you might not expect.

MAKING FACES

Our emotions elicit an array of expressions on our own faces,
from the nearly imperceptible to the obvious that can appear
and disappear within fractions of a second (125 to 200 mil-
liseconds).[17] Despite the speed and subtlety of these changes,
people are equipped from birth to recognize and mimic them.
Researchers have found that soon after they are born infants
will copy an experimenter's facial gestures.[18] Stick out your
tongue, purse your lips, or open your mouth and a baby will
too. When their mothers make happy sounds and faces, their
babies return the same expressions. What's more, it works the
other way around. Mothers imitate their babies' expression of
emotion as well.[19]

Mimicry is not limited to facial expressions, but extends
to speech and movement as well. In conversation people very
quickly copy each other's accent, speech rate, and vocal intensity. Before long they are using the same tone of voice and set-
tle on a common rhythm. From how long they speak to how
long they pause, people copy their conversation partner.[20] As if
singing, conversations become duets as people deftly inte-
grate their parts. And they are dancing too. As they speak,
people adopt the other's posture and gestures, sympathetically
adjusting their bodies moment by moment to synchrony in
what's called postural echo.[21]

Mimicry, scientists argue, is communication, conveying a rapid and precise nonverbal message to another person."[22] This isn't merely active listening, the conscious and sometimes disingenuous attempt to convince someone that we are paying attention. It is unintentional and far more subtle. It's an automatic response hardwired into every person. And while such motor mimicry may start young, it's not limited to children or to a tiny collection of expressions. People of all ages imitate everything from facial expressions to speech, involving the full range of human emotions.

Observational learning, as we've seen, is more effective when we are like the person setting the example. By copying another person's posture, speech, and facial expressions during conversation, motor mimicry enhances observational learning and ensures that we become ever more like each of the people with whom we interact.

At first it seems that motor mimicry during conversation demonstrates only that it is possible to catch each other's physical expressions of emotion, not the emotion itself.[23] And this would be true if all emotions arose internally and your furrowed brow, clenched fist, and a raised voice was merely the physical manifestation of your anger. By this view, emotions operate only from the inside out. First we feel them; then we express them. But it also works the other way around. Researchers have found that "we may come to feel an intense emotion as we simulate emotional expressions or behavior."[24] You smile when you are happy, but smiling also *makes* you happy just as frowning makes you sad. By trying on an emotion's posture or facial expression, we can also don the emotion itself.

To test this notion a group of German psychologists devised a study in which subjects were shown cartoons while holding a pen in one of two ways. One group clinched it between their teeth, which made them smile by contracting the two major smiling muscles in their face. The other group held it between their lips, an arrangement that had the opposite effect. The people made to smile found the cartoons much funnier. "In the facial-feedback system," wrote Malcolm Gladwell in Annals of Psychology, in *The New Yorker,* "an expression you do not even know that you have can create an emotion you did not choose to feel."[25]

It follows that if we can read people's expressions with enough speed and accuracy to copy them ourselves, then we might also be able to tell when their facial expression don't match their stated feelings. If a person tells a lie, for instance, their face might still tell the truth, thereby allowing us to quickly identify those who don't really mean what they were saying. By mimicking their facial expressions we would come to feel their emotion and the dissonance created by their lie. In fact, this is precisely what happens.

The human face can make forty-three distinct muscle movements, which are called action units. Because many can occur at the same time, the possible combinations number near ten thousand. Many of these are nonsensical combinations of the kind you get by wildly contorting your face. But in 1978 a pair of researchers, Paul Ekman and Wallace Friesen, identified about three thousand that seemed to mean something and that together account for the fundamental catalog of human emotion.[26] The researchers recorded the various combinations, along with tips for recognizing and interpreting them in a document they called the "Facial Action Coding System," or FACS (pronounced, "face"), a resource later consulted by the likes of Pixar and DreamWorks to improve the believability of the facial expressions made by animated characters.

Their research revealed that combinations of both voluntary and involuntary muscles produce facial expressions accompanying many human emotions. A genuine smile, for example, involves cheek muscles within your control that lift the corners of your mouth, but also muscles around your eyes you cannot consciously command. As a consequence, your face has a mind of its own and often betrays those emotions you really feel while preventing you from falsifying the ones you don't. "Our voluntary expressive system is the way we intentionally signal our emotions," writes Malcolm Gladwell. "But our involuntary expressive system is in many ways even more important: it is the way we . . . signal our authentic feelings."[27] Scientists like Ekman agree. "I don't think mating and infatuation and friendships and closeness would occur if our faces didn't work that way."[28] Neither would phenomena like *The Passion of the Christ* or *The Purpose-Driven® Life*, because they depend on people's ability to accurately express and interpret genuine, positive emotions like affection, excitement, and satisfaction.

This discovery also helps explain why people routinely say that personal recommendations influence their purchase decisions more than advertising. The woman in a detergent commercial is an actress—pretending to be someone she's not while attempting to express emotions she doesn't actually feel. How could she communicate with the same potency and power as a neighbor who just used that new detergent to remove a stain from her favorite shirt? Advertising is far colder than personal recommendation—a fake smile in a photograph compared with the searing heat released by the contagious joy of a customer evangelist.

If contagious emotions enhance the power of personal recommendation, then the next question is: how do we tap into the process by which they spread? Several factors contribute.

SENDING

Psychologists have found that people vary in their ability to experience and/or express emotion, giving some a higher heat release rate than the general population and making them more effective at spreading the fire.[29] In *The Tipping Point*, Malcolm Gladwell writes about people he calls Salesmen, whose outgoing nature and gregarious behavior makes them more emotionally expressive than their peers.[30]

This revelation sent many marketers scurrying to identify Salesmen in hopes of recruiting them as customer evangelists for their products. But that may be unnecessary because studies have also shown that while certain people are, in fact, more expressive than others, the difference only matters in relation to their ability to spread negative emotions. Salesmen are quick to share their fears, anxieties, and anger with those they meet, but virtually *everyone*, expressive or not, seems capable of spreading their happiness.[31] The one exception is for gender, not facial structure. Women are more emotionally expressive than men. "They spontaneously smile and laugh more, engage in more eye contact, touch more, and show more body movement," wrote the authors of one study. "Even when men and women are both *trying* to communicate nonverbally, women are the far more effective senders" (emphasis added).[32]

Expressive people may have an edge when it comes to spreading negative emotions, but there is little difference among people when it comes to expressing the positive variety that spreads marketing fires. Expressing our emotions, however, is only half the story. Emotional contagion depends equally on people's receptivity, and here personal differences are more striking. Our susceptibility to catching positive emotions varies depending on several factors, including whether we are a man or woman, are paying attention to or ignoring others, the extent to which we derive our self-identity from membership in groups, and our emotional attachment to those sending the emotions.

RECEIVING

Several factors profoundly influence our susceptibility to "catching" other people's emotions, but once again women have a slight advantage. A review of more than 125 different studies found that women were modestly better at judging emotional states.[33] The major factors determining our susceptibility to emotional contagion, however, are more mental than physical—having perhaps as much to do with our situation and attitude as with our sex or the number of muscles in our face. Our ability to "observationally learn" someone's emotion is a function of our behavior and our environment.

ATTENTION

Only by paying attention can we notice that the riders on the elevator are facing the rear or that we are drifting farther from other runners on the track; likewise emotions are caught only by those who attend to their surroundings. Women may be better at catching emotion because they are better at paying attention. In conversation, they establish eye contact faster, more often, and for longer periods than men.[34] For both men and women, though, the attention we give often depends on the emotion being expressed. People don't like bad news. While they will closely concentrate on positive information, they pay less attention to the unsettling, sometimes to the point of blocking it altogether.

BELONGING

People who derive their sense of self from their membership in a group often catch emotions from its members. Christians sacrifice a measure of individuality when they join a church and become part of the "body of believers." And men, especially, are notorious for blurring the lines between identity and occupation. Ask a man who he is and he may reply with his job title. From diabetics to cancer survivors, from Packers fans to sorority sisters, people feel a special bond because they derive a portion of their identity from the group to which they belong.

Be careful, though, because not all groups qualify. Only those from which people derive a "sense of self" make the cut. People can be taxpayers, commuters, baby boomers, or frequent fliers without thinking of themselves in those terms and unless they do, their membership in that group will not increase their susceptibility to emotional contagion.

The size of the group also enhances its ability to influence our emotional state. Smaller groups have a larger influence because it is easier for people to feel integrally involved.

LIKING AND LIKENESS

The stronger the emotional bond, the better the emotional connection. Friends, family, and lovers are especially prone to catching each other's emotions. This makes perfect sense when you consider the importance of attention and belonging. We pay close attention to the people we like, thereby enhancing our ability to catch what they are sending. Since a true bond of friendship is usually only possible between people of roughly equal status, emotional contagion is also governed, in part, by our similarity to other people.[35]

FORTY DAYS OF SHARED EMOTIONS

The Forty Days of Purpose Campaign fanned its flames by providing nearly perfect conditions for emotional contagion.

- The program's design assured that people paid attention during sermons and weekly small group discussions.
- Six out of every ten people attending church were women, emotion's most effective senders and receivers.
- Churches tend to draw membership from their immediate surroundings and so congregations reflected the common ethnicity and social status of the neighboring community.
- Not only were churchgoers alike, they also liked each other. Beyond developing friendships as they worshiped together, Christians were commanded to love one another.
- Not surprisingly, their sense of belonging, to their faith and to each other, was very strong. The first question and answer in the Heidelberg Catechism, a summary of Christian doctrine, demonstrates the degree to which many Christians construe their identity with their faith.
  - Question: What is your only comfort in life and death?
  - Answer: That I am not my own, but belong with body and soul, both in life and in death, to my faithful Savior Jesus Christ.
- Finally, about ninety people attend the average American church service,[36] a number that provided an ideal balance of size and intimacy.

The degree to which people can spread their positive feelings about your product to those around them has more to do with the place than the person. Situations make the Salesman, so stop searching for *contagious people* and look instead for *contagious circumstances.* Introducing your product into smaller groups of similar people who share a strong emotional attachment to each other and the group can dramatically improve the speed with which it diffuses through that community and beyond. Leveraging the conditions that enable social learning and emotional contagion fans the flames and spreads information, emotion, and your product from one person to the next.

The ability of one person to influence another is powerful and well understood. Just how individual influence expands to affect whole populations, though, was a mystery for many years. Why did some trends catch on while others failed? The new science of networks is beginning to unravel the mystery.

NETWORKS

It is impossible to understand how individual behavior aggregates to collective behavior, how the flame from a single match can become a forest fire, or how a phenomenon like *The Purpose-Driven® Life* can spread from one California minister to twenty million readers, without understanding networks and their behavior. The same forces that synchronize a clapping crowd at a rock concert or flashing fireflies in Asia are responsible for social coordination too.

We can spread information to other people only if we have some contact with them. Those people we encounter and associate with during our life comprise our social network and social networks are the conduit through which personal influence propagates.[37]

"Agency" is the word sociologists use to describe our personal characteristics—that complex amalgam of experience, interests, knowledge, and tastes that drives our choices.

Though we expect agency to influence what goes into our cart at the supermarket, it also has a profound effect on the universe of people we may eventually meet. It's nice to think we choose our friends directly, but that's not quite right. More often we choose to join particular groups or to participate in certain contexts based on our interests. That association, in turn, brings us into contact with people who share our interests and later become our friends.

Just as the competing desires to race ahead and to avoid burning out cause runners to cluster on a track, two seemingly contradictory desires influence whom we gather with. Each of us wants to pursue our individual interests (agency), but we also want to fit in. Those competing desires move us to find and join communities of interest called affiliation networks. Affiliation networks allow us to pursue our interests *and* belong to a group. The more affiliation networks two people share, say, by attending the same high school and joining the same gym, the closer they become. Common context comes first. The bond of friendship arises later. This is important because it means we always have something in common with the people in our social network and that commonality is what directs and encourages the spread of information.

Minimally, all networks contain nodes, links, and clusters. In a social network, every person is a node and every relationship is a link. People you know directly form your network neighborhood, and clusters are formed by groups of people who all know each other. I know my six buddies from high school, for instance, and they also know each other. Together we form an affiliation network based on our common high school experience and a cluster because we all know each other.

Every person participates in several affiliation networks, which together define their social identity. Each person's big world, then, is the sum total of their many little worlds. My social network, just like yours, consists of many small over-lapping communities that are densely internally connected and that overlap by virtue of my multiple affiliations. For example, in addition to my friends from high school, I have a cluster of friends at work and a cluster of Packers buddies. I am the common participant who links my work, high school, and Packers clusters, causing them to overlap by sharing information among them and by occasionally introducing a friend from one cluster to a friend from another.

The dense, short links within a cluster—between a person and their friends—are strong ties that help information spread quickly and effectively within affiliation networks. But our social networks include weak ties too; these are mere acquaintances, with whom we may share information, but have little in common, like a seatmate on an airplane. Weak ties, those chance encounters with people from other social spheres, make it possible for information to jump beyond our affiliation networks and into others like a spark lifted by the wind from a forest fire that starts a new blaze in another loca-tion. Trends and social phenomena depend upon both strong *and* weak ties.

FLASHOVER

Flashover is the goal of every PyroMarketer; it is that moment when the tiny fire you began with the driest tinder leaps beyond the initial group to ignite whole populations. The social equivalent is called an information cascade and net-work experts now know it depends on two factors: a low threshold and appropriate connectivity. Threshold refers to a person's ignition temperature. How likely are they to switch from being a prospect to being a customer by adopting an idea, product, or trend? The lower a person's ignition temperature or threshold, the more vulnerable they are.

Connectivity measures the size of a person's social network. How many people do they know? With whom can they share the message? Surprisingly, more connections are *not* necessarily better. In fact, too much connectivity can kill an information cascade. This is because it is the percentage of nodes in our network neighborhood that adopt a new product, not the absolute number, that determines whether someone else's choice will influence ours. Think of the man on the elevator. Two-thirds and even three-quarters of the riders did not sway his decision to face the front. It wasn't until four-fifths of his network neighborhood faced the rear that he also turned. However, if the elevator held one hundred riders—if, in effect, the rider had one hundred friends instead of four—then the four facing the rear would be a tiny minority of the network neighborhood and would exert little influence.

Information cascades rely on a trade-off between threshold and connectivity. To imagine how it works, let's consider an example using this book. Suppose a person needs to see 25 percent of their network neighborhood buy a new business book before they adopt it themselves. A person with one friend (low connectivity) becomes vulnerable to buying that book, no matter how high their ignition temperature, the moment their friend buys because a recommendation from that one friend represents the unanimous choice of their entire social network. Such a person would almost certainly buy, but the cascade would end because, with just one friend, they could not spread the message to anyone else.

A person with one hundred friends (high connectivity) is no more helpful, but for a different reason. They have too many contacts and the odds are slim that enough of their friends (twenty-five) will buy the book to influence their choice. With too few recommendations they never buy.

Affiliation networks are the key to starting information cascades because they provide the ideal balance between threshold and connectivity, what's called a vulnerable cluster. A vulnerable cluster is a group of people who know each other and that contains at least one person whose ignition temperature is lower than the heat of your marketing and one or more additional people whose ignition temperature is within the reach of a single personal recommendation. Your marketing lights the person with the lowest ignition point. They, in turn, influence a couple more, who, thanks to their larger numbers, influence the others via social proof. Because people join multiple, overlapping groups, your marketing fire quickly spreads as they take its message to their other affiliation networks. Weak ties help it to jump even greater distances.

This is what happened with *The Purpose-Driven® Life*. The campaign began in affiliation networks created by a handful of churches. By dividing each congregation into small groups of eight to ten that met once each week, the campaign created network neighborhoods of ideal size and ensured that if three or four people adopted the book and its message, the rest of the group would soon follow. The four hundred thousand people in those initial churches became excited about the book and began recommending it in their other affiliation networks: their work, their school, their subdivision, their golf league, and so on. Those people took the news to their networks. Some people took their book on business trips and talked about it with their seatmate on the plane. That person bought a copy and began sharing it with their network neighborhood in another city. Soon whole communities were synchronized.

FUTURISTIC MARKETING?

Imagine the ideal marketing campaign. A highly advanced program boasting technologies you have only dreamed about. What would it be like?

Such a plan would know exactly who to approach without being told. You would release it into the world and it would automatically, and with very few errors, find those people most likely to want and benefit from your offering. Your plan would have built a communications infrastructure to transport your message to those people most likely to buy. The ideal plan would discern subtle differences among people, suggesting one product to some while recommending something else to others. Beyond knowing whom to target, it would also calculate precisely when to approach them, choosing just the right moment to deliver its message. It wouldn't interrupt people's dinner, or talk to them when they were angry. Instead it would introduce your product at the moment of a person's greatest need—suggesting WD-40 when their door hinge squeaked or Tide just after they stained their shirt.

The ideal marketing campaign would continually adjust its message, optimizing its relevance and persuasiveness for each recipient. When the sale called for a demonstration, it would give one. When a gentle recommendation was sufficient, it would do that.

It would also make sure people received your message. If they didn't, it would restate it as many times as necessary, but no more, until each person understood. It would accurately read and interpret feedback from the consumer and adjust accordingly. Such a campaign would even displace your competitor's message, giving you exclusive access to each communications channel. It would cost little or nothing, be self-replicating, and endure without end.

Does it sound too good to be true? I am not describing futuristic technology still decades away or the wishful thinking of a fertile imagination. I just described the latent power possessed by your customers. And it's a power you can begin using today by fanning the flames. Now that you know the principles, it's time to consider some specific tactics.

1. **Start with the Driest Tinder.** They are an affiliation network of ideal size and susceptibility. By promoting to people most likely to buy your product just as they are gathering with like-minded friends, you make it possible to dominate a group and create the conditions for an information cascade.

2. **Increase Their Connectivity—After They Buy.** Too much connectivity is only a threat to an information cascade before someone buys. Once they convert, you want to connect them as broadly as possible. By building communities where customers and prospects can gather, you create new affiliation networks through which influence can propagate. *Fast Company* magazine has local chapters of readers called the Fast Company of Friends who gather to celebrate their common love for the popular business magazine. What can you do that's similar?

3. **Extend Their Reach.** People influence those they can touch. Left alone they will tell their neighbors and close friends. But, if you give them the tools, they will tell distant relatives and long-lost high school buddies. E-mail is great, but there are other ideas too. In addition to a warranty card, what about a postage-paid mailer people can use to tell friends they just bought your product? To promote a book on child rearing, I once sent copies (touch them with the match) to Christian family counselors (dri-

est tinder) and included a pad of fifty prescription slips that made it easier for them to recommend the book to their clients (fan the flames).

4. **Divide and Conquer.** Information spreads best through smaller groups. If the driest tinder for your product gathers in large groups, how can you organize them into smaller clusters through which information is more likely to spread? What about replacing your national ad campaign with a series of smaller regional efforts?

5. **May I Have Your Attention?** People buy products after watching other people enjoy using them. Try reading this book in public and watch how many people ask you about it. Soon you'll be fanning the flames for *PyroMarketing.* How can you get people to use your product or service in public? Sometimes it's a simple as suggesting it.

6. **Help Them Belong.** Do your customers just buy your product, or do they feel a part of something bigger? Fans of the Green Bay Packers have had the opportunity to buy stock in the team. Stockholders receive special catalogs with Packers stockholder clothing only they can buy. If you help your customers feel special, they won't be able to resist telling their friends.

7. **Build Community.** Ideas grow and develop in social communities. If your customers or prospects don't gather naturally, look for ways to help them. Often it's quite simple.

Most banquet speeches are the same. You eat your lunch with about seven strangers and make small talk about whatever you find in common. Then the speaker takes the podium and talks for about twenty minutes before the meeting breaks up and people go their separate ways. But it doesn't have to be that way. When Lee Strobel, author of *The Case for a Cre-*

ator, spoke to the Religion News Writers Association, I rearranged the meeting so that he spoke first and the lunch was last. This simple change meant that as the religion reporters from newspapers across the country ate their lunch their conversation turned to the one thing they had in common—the content of the message Lee had just given. Instead of talking about sports, the weather, or travel nightmares, their conversation focused on Lee's argument for intelligent design. By discussing his message they reinforced it in their own minds. Not surprisingly, those reporters later wrote a higher percentage of columns on Lee's talk than on the talks of other speakers.

When a prospect buys, they don't just become a customer. By fanning the flames they'll become a customer evangelist—an unpaid addition to your sales and marketing staff capable of exponentially expanding the reach of your marketing. Learning how to create them is vital to your success, but so is learning how to keep them. It's time to save the coals.

CHAPTER SUMMARY

People spread messages more effectively than advertising. The driest tinder will buy based solely on their personal preferences and knowledge of the options, but everyone else turns to decision externalities—paying attention to the other runners on their social track in order to make the best decision. Through observational learning some will decide to buy or avoid your product based on other people's experience. Others will feel the pressure of social proof and buy your product as a growing percentage of their friends do. Still others, caught up in emotion, will buy on the strength of a friend's recommendation. Whether your product reaches flashover depends on a trade-off between threshold

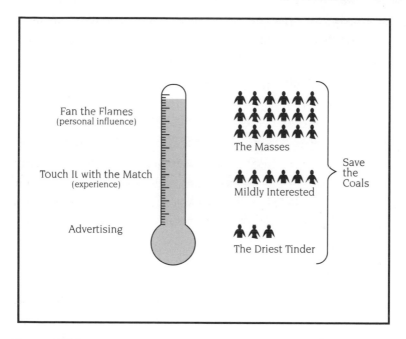

Figure 5.2 Personal influence generates more heat than marketing and experience. Finding ways to leverage its power through your existing customers is the only way to reach the masses.

and connectivity in the social network through which it spreads. You can enhance its chances by promoting to the driest tinder and its natural affiliation networks and by enhancing each customer's connectivity just after they buy.

FLASHPOINTS

1. Does the complexity of your product or the number of competing choices make your best prospects uncertain? Who do they turn to for advice when they cannot decide? How can you equip those recommenders to influence their friends for your product or service?

2. Divide your customer list into those who can make the right purchase decision on their own and those who need the help of externalities. Devise marketing plans optimized for each group and their needs.

3. Can you help people use your product in public? Can you encourage them to use it in the presence of similar people? Find groups where they congregate and allow the entire group to try your product or service.

4. How can you encourage people to smile while trying your product or taking in its advertising? By acting happy they'll soon be happy and come to associate that positive emotion with your company and its offerings.

5. Do your customers feel a sense of belonging? Do they derive a sense of their personal identity from using your product or being a member of the group of people that does? Can you create such a group?

6. Are your customers members of any affiliation networks? Can you reach them with your marketing messages while they are in those groups? What tools would encourage them to talk about your product or service with their network neighbors?

6

Save the Coals

Fire; when once you have kindled it you may easily
preserve it, but if you have extinguished it, you will find it an
arduous task to rekindle it again.
—Socrates

The unusually long evolution of the match began in 1669 when an alchemist, trying to transform base metals into gold, produced phosphorus instead and failed to realize that he had created gold of a different sort. In 1680, Englishman Robert Boyle began to understand the chemical's value when he discovered that sulfur and phosphorus burst into flames when rubbed together. The technology lay dormant for almost 150 years until the English pharmacist John Walker created what he called sulphuretted peroxide strikables, the large and cumbersome forerunner of the modern match. Some years later, in 1889, a Philadelphia lawyer named Joshua Pusey gave the world a portable, reliable way to make fire by inventing the first paper match book. Ironically, his invention didn't "catch on" until 1895, when, to promote the New York opening of the Mendelson Opera Company, the cast advertising on the outside of his matchbooks.[1] Perhaps the link between fire and marketing was inevitable.

The people of earth strike more than five hundred billion matches each year, quickly making fires and not giving much thought to how difficult the task can be without them. Throughout history the acquisition of fire brought the need to preserve it. It is far easier to maintain a fire, or rekindle one you've already built, than to start one from scratch. In the old days people preserved their fires with a curfew, a brass "fire cover" that was placed over coals that had been raked together. (Covering the fire effectively ended social gatherings for the night, hence the modern meaning of the word.) To light the next fire, the coals were placed near some tinder and blown by bellows until the tinder burst into flame. Before the new fire died, some coals were again set aside and covered in order to repeat the process the next day. Prior to the invention of matches, smart people saved the coals, and so must you.

In PyroMarketing, saving the coals means keeping a record of the people who respond to your marketing so you can identify, understand, engage, and mobilize them for years to come. That is how your marketing builds equity. If you know and understand your customers—who they are, where they live, and what they love—then you can quickly and affordably engage them with relevant messages about new products. With one fire secured, you can use new matches to grow your business by building additional fires. Most important, a record of your customers allows you to build relationships and begin transforming promiscuous shoppers into loyal customer evangelists who are eager to promote your business to the people along their social network. By saving the coals today, you ensure your ability to build new marketing fires tomorrow—without wasting valuable matches.

Saving the coals is the final step in the PyroMarketing process, but in some ways it is also the first. By keeping a record of your customers and prospects, their preferences, behavior, and purchase-related data, you enable the other three steps in the process. This is what makes PyroMarketing a repeatable, growth-oriented marketing strategy. A database helps you quickly identify the driest tinder for a new product and contact them to provide a personal experience or to encourage word of mouth.

Rick Warren could enlist twelve hundred pastors to participate in the Forty Days of Purpose Campaign with a single e-mail message because he had built a database of—and a relationship with—the seventy thousand pastors who used his www.pastors.com Web site. By saving the coals as the last step in a previous campaign, he enabled the first step in the next.

The marketing team for *The Passion of the Christ* kept a record of the churches that supported the theatrical release by promoting it to their community or by taking their entire church to see the film. When the home video version became available, they sold the film by the case to those same churches by mailing each of them a single postcard.

Unlike PyroMarketing, mass marketing often keeps no record of its customers and instead uses large, expensive advertising campaigns to find buyers for each new product. It lures consumers from the masses with promotions, but lets them slip anonymously back into the crowd after they buy. Without a record of their customers, companies that use mass marketing are forever starting over because they must spend each new advertising budget to find many of the same people who bought the last time. Expensive and inefficient, mass marketing uses new matches to rebuild the same fire. You simply can't support a growing business with such a wasteful strategy.

Most businesses expect their sales and profits to increase year after year. Yet those same companies often don't increase their marketing budgets at a comparable rate. If you are expected to grow your sales with stagnant marketing budgets— if the number of fires you must build exceeds the number of matches you're given—then you have no choice but to save the coals.

The growth of your business depends on sales but sales depend on customers. To succeed, you must know who they are and how to serve them. That is where database marketing can help. "Database marketing and the World Wide Web are not just ways to increase profits by reducing costs and selling more products and services, although those things are, and must be, the primary results," says database marketing expert and author of *Strategic Database Marketing*, Arthur M. Hughes. "Rather, database marketing and the web are tools that provide management with customer information. That information is used in various ways to increase customer retention and increase customer acquisition rates—the essence of business strategy."[2]

Mass marketing focuses solely on customer acquisition, but that is a losing strategy. According to Paul Wang, associate professor of marketing at Northwestern University, $100 spent on acquiring a new customer nets about $50 in profits. Trading dollars for fifty-cent pieces is not an approach you can sustain for long, nor would you want to. Marketing, like fire, should be about more than acquisition. Acquiring *and* preserving customers is the focus of PyroMarketing and the strategy that makes the most fiscal sense. According to Wang, $100 spent on customer retention nets about $150 in profits.[3] Which do you prefer?

DATABASE BENEFITS

As your database allows you to build relationships with your customers, you will reap several positive outcomes.

1. **Improved Retention Rate.** As you build relationships with your customers, you will also increase their loyalty.
2. **Better Customers.** As you dialogue with your customers, you educate them. As they learn more about your company and its products, their stock of knowledge increases and their need for decision externalities decreases. Smart and self-sufficient consumers shift from imitators to initiators—from the masses to the driest tinder. As you nurture the relationship, you lower the customer's ignition temperature, making them more likely to act on your advertising without the need for experience or personal influence.
3. **Improved Relationships.** As customers come to know and trust you, your business becomes an extension of their social network. If they can't decide for themselves what product or service to buy, they may turn to you for advice.
4. **Increased Sales.** Loyal customers spend more. A database helps you identify your best customers and their interests so that you can better target them with relevant offers. It also helps you identify opportunities for cross-marketing that can lead to increased sales.
5. **Reduced Costs.** A consumer database can reduce the cost of promoting and delivering your product. Direct marketing to high-quality customers you know by name is more efficient than mass marketing to strangers. Expect your promotional costs to decline as your database grows.

A percentage of your customers may also begin buying from you directly, if that is your business model, reducing your distribution costs.

6. **Better Referrals.** A consumer database helps you identify customer evangelists and equip them to spread your message to their friends. What's more, research has shown that referred customers are more loyal and also spend more than customers acquired through traditional advertising.

By now you may be convinced of the need to save the coals. If so, then it's time to concentrate on the process itself.

WHO IS YOUR CUSTOMER?

The first question you must answer before building a customer database is, who is my customer? This may seem like a silly question, but taking it lightly will hurt your results.

By customer I am referring to the buyer or end user of your product or service. If you are a publisher, then your customer is the reader. If you run a lawn service, your customer is the person who owns the grass. "But my company sells its products through retailers," you say. "The retailer knows the consumer. We don't need to." Oh yes you do. It's important to know your retail customers so you can build relationships and serve them, but ultimately the end user matters most. Even if retailers love your company, they won't carry your product for long unless consumers are buying it. Conversely, if consumers demand your product, then retailers will carry it even if your relationship is less than ideal. Now, obviously, you should try to build positive relationships with both retailers and end consumers. My point is simply that you cannot ignore the end user just because you have good retail relationships. You dare not entrust that relationship to another company.

Some retailers believe they own the relationship with the consumer and resent manufacturers who market to them directly. Though it may take some time, this fallacy can be overcome by gently, but persistently, educating your retail partners. First of all, no one "owns" the relationship with the consumer, except maybe the consumer. Just because you have captured some of a person's personal data does not mean you have captured them. Consumers have relationships with many people, products, companies, and retail outlets and make or break them at their pleasure. If you doubt me, call any consumer on your database (if you already have one) and ask them if you own the relationship. You'll hear laughter if they don't hang up first.

Second, when a consumer buys something, they make at least two decisions: a product decision and a channel decision. The product decision involves what to buy. The channel decision determines where they will buy it. Manufacturers should concentrate their marketing on the product decision and retailers should focus their marketing on the channel decision. By sharing information from your databases and working together, you can achieve a one-two punch that satisfies consumers while selling your product through the retailer's stores. Smart companies create a win-win situation with their retail partners by sharing this data. Keep a record of how this collaboration improves each business's performance and use that story to convince the more reluctant.

Before moving on, let's pause to clarify something. The terms *retailer, customer,* and *consumer* can get confusing. To keep things clear, from this point forward I will assume you are a manufacturer or a service provider and refer to the end user as "the consumer."

TRUST

The key to your consumer database is trust. It allows you to build, fill, and increase your database. It enables you to improve the value of your customers and increase both revenues and profits. It is by far the most important ingredient because a consumer database is only as good as the data it stores, and people won't give you their information or their business unless they trust you. Building a relationship of trust is a prerequisite for any database marketing program and the recipe for its healthy maintenance. Earning your customer's trust begins by first earning the trust of your employees. Most often they are the point of contact between your business and its customers. If you keep the promises you've made to your people, they will be ambassadors for your organization's character and able to personally vouch for that trustworthiness with customers.

The relationship between trust and your database is symbiotic. Just as a consumer's trust in your company helps you build a database, your database can help you build consumer trust. Trust, according to *Merriam-Webster's Collegiate Dictionary*, is the "assured reliance on the character, ability, strength, or truth of someone or something."[4] Trust, therefore, is about meeting expectations. Meeting expectations, however, depends on first knowing what is expected. What kind of character do consumers expect from your company? What is their expectation of your firm's truthfulness, or abilities, or strength? Why not ask? Your database enables a dialogue with consumers that can help answer these questions and allow you to align deliverables with the consumer's expectations, creating trust as the product.

Perhaps it's best not to overanalyze the issue of trust. After all, when it comes to your most trusting relationships, you probably haven't thought twice about how to achieve that confidence. It happened naturally. That's because trust is really pretty simple. When you care about someone else as much or more than you care about yourself, you will routinely overdeliver on their expectations. Often, in that environment, the other person reciprocates and, as each party repeatedly gets more than they bargained for from every encounter, trust blossoms and grows. Instead of trying to figure out how to win your customer's trust, try imagining your customers as friends you are trying to help. If you really care about meeting their needs, and back it up with your behavior, then trust will naturally follow—and so will sales.

BUILDING YOUR DATABASE

If your company already has a consumer database, then let me congratulate you for your vision and willingness to invest for the long term. If you don't yet have a database, then it's time you built one.

Databases can be complex, but they don't have to be. Financial services companies trying to analyze rapid-fire ticker feeds need sophisticated databases capable of processing thousands of transactions per second. You just need a place to keep track of your customers and their behavior—at least initially. Don't wait until you become an expert. You will miss hundreds of days and thousands of valuable customer records waiting to acquire the expertise you think you need. It's better to simply get started using whatever knowledge and skills you possess and learn the rest as you go.

Your first database can be quite simple. If it takes you more than a year to build, then it is probably too complex. There are a number of affordable database programs from Microsoft Access to Filemaker Pro that are simple enough for the novice yet powerful enough to grow with your company's needs. You can start simply and, as your knowledge and expertise grow, begin to access the program's more sophisticated features. Whether you do it yourself or hire an outside firm doesn't really matter, as long as you get started right away.

You are building a database in order to know, understand, engage, and mobilize consumers. The information you choose to record should facilitate those goals.

There are really only two types of information you can know about a consumer: who they are (demographics) and what they do (behavior).[5] Basic demographic information can help you better know your customer. This can involve recording information you typically associate with consumer databases, things like gender, date of birth, education, income/financial situation, home ownership, and whether they have children. Depending on the nature of your business, you may want to record their clothing size, the kind of car they drive, or their color preferences. Try to collect information that will improve the service you are able to provide.

You can't serve consumers if you can't reach them so be sure to track their contact information, including title, first name, last name, address, city, state, zip-plus-four, phone, e-mail address, cell phone, and more. However, it is not enough to know how to reach your consumers. You must also have permission to contact them and know how they want to be reached. Knowing their phone number does not give you permission to call them. Ask your consumers how they want to hear from you—and how often. If you respect them with your marketing, they'll be as satisfied with your promotions as they are with your product or service.

The best predictor of future behavior is past behavior and so *understanding* your consumers requires knowing what they do. What organizations or clubs have they joined? To which organizations do they donate money or time? Think of those activities that reveal passions or interests related to your product or service and record them.

Be careful not to ask for too much, too soon. Don't expect them to marry you on the first date. Instead, start by asking for enough information to continue the relationship and build it from there. Consumers are increasingly protective of their personal data, and rightly so. Identity theft is a serious crime and it's on the rise. Don't expect intimacy if you've just met. People won't divulge any of their personal data until they trust and trust takes time.

Whenever possible, record consumers' purchase behavior, including what they buy, when they buy, and how much they spend. Recency, frequency, and monetary data, as they are called, will be important to crafting database marketing strategies that maximize ROI and improve customer profitability. Knowing why they buy is also helpful. Are they giving your product as a gift? Gift givers are tremendous customer evangelists. It is far more efficient to encourage a single person who buys gifts for ten than to try, through your marketing, to convince those ten people to buy your product for themselves.

Capture the information generated by every transaction. Think about how you can use it to build a relationship with your customer. A mobile disc jockey firm called Thunder & Lighting entertained at wedding receptions. As a result, it knew each client's wedding date and sent a card congratulating them on their one-year anniversary. Not only did this thoughtful tactic build a relationship with the consumer but, because newlyweds often have friends who are dating or engaged, it quickly generated new business too. Thunder & Lighting didn't try to sell; instead it served by recognizing and congratulating its customers. That act, however, enhanced the company image and reminded its clients of its excellent service. Recommendations and new business naturally followed.

Some information is especially helpful to the PyroMarketing process and is important to capture and record. Knowing how you acquired a customer, for example, can suggest something about their value. Did they respond to your advertising, to a personal experience, or were they referred by someone? Did they require the influence of all three before deciding to buy? Does it cost more to market to certain people than you earn when they finally buy? Are some customers far more profitable than others? Knowing the answer will help you identify each customer's ignition temperature as it relates to the product or service they bought and understand how to interact with that customer in the future.

It is also useful to learn and record a customer's recommendation behavior. Do they recommend? How actively? What kind of customers do they bring you? By keeping track you can identify customer evangelists and equip them for effectiveness. Remember, a customer's value is not measured by their purchase behavior alone, but also by the new sales and customers they prompt through their recommendations. You may find that some customers personally buy very little, but are indirectly responsible for considerable revenues and profits thanks to their vigorous referrals and recommendations. Think of these people as an extension of your sales department. You measure your salespeople according to how many sales they generate, not by how much they personally buy. Measure the value of certain customers the same way.

By knowing which customers buy for themselves and which recommend to others, you can devise appropriate strategies. You may touch one group with the match to encourage additional purchases while fanning the flames with the other group by equipping them with tools that help them recommend.

FILL YOUR DATABASE

Every new promotion is an opportunity to meet new consumers, learn more about them, and store the results. As you design new marketing plans, look for ways to collect consumer data. Every one of your future campaigns should include a way to capture and record consumer data. The Internet can make this easy. Here are examples that may trigger some ideas.

- If your company offers discounts, switch from coupons to rebates. Coupons tell you nothing about the consumer that used them, but rebate forms can collect whatever data you like. Not only will rebate redemption firms like Continental Promotions Group. (www.cpginc.com) send checks to deserving consumers, they will also provide you with electronic copies of consumer data from each rebate form. You get consumer contact information and can profile them further as someone who responds to discount offers.
- If you use coupons, try dispensing them from a Web site by asking a consumer to register with their contact information before downloading the coupon. You gain control over how many coupons you distribute, you can better calculate redemption rates as a percentage of the total universe of coupons, and you build a database of interested prospects.
- If you advertise in magazines, look for publications with reader response cards or ask your favorite publications to begin offering the service. These cards allow readers to request more information on advertised products. The magazine forwards these requests to you. It's one way for your print advertising to generate actual sales leads.
- I promoted the book *The Case for a Creator* by Lee Strobel with a Web site (www.caseforacreator.com) that allowed people to

become members. In no time I had collected e-mail addresses for hundreds of people passionate about intelligent design. I sent them e-mail messages with breaking news stories related to intelligent design that linked them back to the site. The members stayed informed, site traffic increased, and I could rally them to promote the book to their social network via e-mail. When The *Case for a Creator Student Edition* was released, I knew exactly where to find the driest tinder and could tell them about the book and encourage them to spread the word without spending a penny of my marketing budget.

- You can read fascinating business articles at www.Forbes.com or thoughtful case studies on direct marketing at www.1to1.com, but only if you register first. By creating a customer profile you gain access to premium content on these helpful business Web sites and they save the coals. Does your company have information your customers want? Would they gladly complete a profile to get it?

- Registering your software gives you access to customer support, but it also provides the software manufacturer with your information. What value-adding services can your company offer customers who register?

- Where does your company touch the consumer directly? Do any of those points of contact give you a chance to save the coals?

- Convert the complainers. Customer complaints offer a great opportunity to save the coals. These people are already giving you a piece of their mind; they might also reveal personal data if it helps resolve their problem. The people who call to complain often make wonderful customer evangelists because they are motivated, passionate, and resourceful. Once you've solved their problem, you may find they are ready to build a positive, lasting relationship with your company.

USING YOUR DATABASE

Just because you have acquired a consumer's information does not mean trust is no longer important. On the contrary, you must continue to earn the consumer's trust for as long as you want a relationship with them. I'm emphasizing this point because a great deal of responsibility comes with a consumer database. Once you know who your customers are and how to contact them, you may be tempted to contact them too often, or to send them messages they haven't requested, or promotions for products that don't really interest them. Don't! A recent Accenture survey asked consumers what compromised trust and 67 percent said aggressive marketing eroded their trust most quickly.[6] An empty consumer database is worthless, but so is one full of data on consumers whose trust you've lost by marketing to them irresponsibly.

LIFETIME VALUE

Concentrating on the driest tinder delivers sales right away. Fanning the flames and saving the coals, however, are strategies that build value over longer periods of time. Your database can prove its worth by helping you determine and track something called lifetime value (LTV). According to database expert Arthur Hughes, lifetime value is "the net present value of the profit that you will realize on the average new customer over a given number of years."[7] It is a way of predicting the future value of your present customers. Lifetime value is not a fixed number. It will change over time, but at any given moment you can take a snapshot of your data and calculate a specific number. Knowing your consumer's lifetime value will help you craft smart marketing strategies and appreciate the wisdom of building long-term relationships.

A lifetime value table will help you with the calculation. Let's look first at a sample table before exploring it point by point. Database expert Arthur M. Hughes created the following example.

LIFETIME CUSTOMER VALUE TABLE

	ACQUISITION YEAR	YEAR 2	YEAR 3
Customers	100,000	60,000	42,000
Retention Rate	60%	70%	80%
Orders per Year	1.8	2.5	3
Average Order Size	$90	$95	$100
Total Revenue	$16,200,000	$14,250,000	$12,600,000
Costs	70%	65%	65%
Cost of Sales	$11,340,000	$9,262,500	$8,190,000
Acquisition/ Marketing Costs	$55	$20	$20
Marketing Costs	$5,500,000	$1,200,000	$840,000
Total Costs	$16,840,000	$10,462,500	$9,030,000
Gross Profit	($640,000)	$3,787,500	$3,570,000
Discount Rate	1	1.16	1.35
Net Present Value	($640,000)	$3,265,086	$2,644,444
Cumulative NPV Profit	($640,000)	$2,625,086	$5,269,531
Customer LTV	($6)	$26	$53

This table uses imaginary numbers, but I encourage you to make your own table and fill it with real numbers from your business. Now let's dig into the data.

In the table above you'll notice that one hundred thousand customers were acquired originally. This figure represents the number of customers captured on the company's database. Notice also that 40 percent of them left after the first year, but that in future years the retention rate improves. That is because retained customers are more loyal than newly acquired customers. It's also true that as customers stay with you, they tend to buy more often and spend more with each purchase. This is an important reason why it is more profitable to retain customers than acquire them.

Our chart assumes the cost of sales is 70 percent, though this figure can vary widely from one business to the next. What seems universally true, however, is that this cost goes down steadily over time because customer service costs to existing customers are typically lower than for newly acquired customers. The longer a customer has been with you, the more they understand about your business and the fewer their questions.

The acquisition/marketing cost is calculated by totaling all of your sales and advertising expenses for the year and dividing that total by the number of newly acquired customers. If you spent a million dollars on sales and marketing, but don't yet have a customer database, then your marketing acquisition cost is $1 million per zero customers acquired. That's not very good. In the example above, sales and marketing totaled $5,500,000 and helped acquire 100,000 new customers: 5,500,000/100,000 = $55. That's quite a bit better.

Our example assumes you spend only $20 per customer on marketing in subsequent years. That money includes both those activities designed to sell as well as those that build your relationship and ensure retention. To calculate gross profit, simply subtract total costs from total revenues.

As I mentioned before, LTV is a forward-looking calculation. As a result, it anticipates profits that will come in over several years. A dollar in hand is worth more than a dollar paid at some future point because of the interest you could have earned by investing it. It is necessary, therefore, to discount future profits in order to determine their present value. The first step is to assign a discount rate. The discount rate (D) is itself a calculated number. You begin with the current market interest rate (i). For our example we will assume it is 8 percent. Next, because no future plans are guaranteed, we will protect ourselves from risk by assigning a risk factor (rf) of 2. Finally, we need the number of years we must wait to receive our anticipated profits (n). To calculate the discount rate for year three, we would use the number 2. Since we are in the acquisition year, the third year is only two years away. The formula looks like this:

$$D = (1 + (i \times rf))^n$$

Now let's do it with real numbers. Assuming 8 percent interest and assigning 2 as our risk factor, the calculation is as follows.

$$D = (1 + (.08 \times 2))^2 \text{ or } D = (1.16)^2 = 1.35$$

Now, to calculate lifetime value (LTV), you simply divide the cumulative net present value (NPV) profits in the third year by the total number of customers acquired in the acquisition year. For our example above, the answer is $52.69 or $53.

LTV rolls up the retention rate, the spending rate, the acquisition, the marketing and goods costs, and the discount rate into a single, wonderful number. This one number helps us quickly see why acquiring new customers—the constant goal of mass marketing—is not a profitable activity and why retaining them, by saving the coals, is. Calculating the average customer LTV for the entire database is important because of what it allows us to do next.

SEGMENT YOUR CUSTOMERS

Not all customers are created equal. Some are much more valuable than others. By segmenting your database you can calculate the LTV of different customer segments and separate the wheat from the chaff. "Economists and accountants often talk as if the main problem of any business is to find the most efficient way to produce products and services. It's not," claims Arthur M. Hughes. "The main problem of any business is to find the most efficient way to sell its products and services. Customers provide the cash flow that keeps any business alive. By building up customer lifetime value, we are building up the key assets of the business—assets that are essential to the survival of the business itself."[8]

Your business needs more than customers; it needs the right customers. It's true that they provide the cash flow that keeps any business alive, but some customers do a better job than others. Just who are the most profitable people? Once you know, you can design promotional campaigns to attract more of them. Without a database, however, you cannot answer this important question.

Consider the various ways you could segment your database in order to reveal the most profitable customer groups. You could segment them by age, sex, income, education, or marital status. You can segment them by how often they shop or how much they spend. You can arrange them according to the affiliation groups they join or by causes to which they donate their money. You can even segment them according to their value as customer evangelists by tracking how often they recommend your company and its products. In fact, you will probably want to slice your data each of those ways and more as you look for the characteristics that define your most profitable customer segments. Which group provides the greatest lifetime value? What traits call them out of the crowd? Which promotions attract the best customers or the hottest evangelists?

Cambridge SoundWorks, a manufacturer of high-quality home electronics, loudspeakers, and home theater equipment calculated the lifetime value of its customers and, after segmenting them, made a surprising discovery. The company, which sells many of its products directly to consumers, had been using its SoundWorks Radio CD740 as an acquisitions tool. The plan was to discount the product to attract new customers hoping they would later upgrade to larger and more expensive home theater systems on which the company made wider margins. What they discovered through their LTV analysis, however, was that customers lured by their offer bought the radio at a deep discount and promptly disappeared.[9] These were not loyal customers CSW could nurture and build; they were one-night stands. By saving the coals and analyzing the results, Cambridge SoundWorks discovered its promotions were perfectly designed to attract the wrong kind of customer.

By analyzing customer data Cambridge SoundWorks separated the chaff, but it also found the wheat. For years CSW thought the best customer for its high-end products bought every component of a large system all at once. What the data revealed, however, was that only about 2 percent of its customers behaved this way. Instead, a more profitable class of consumer emerged from their analysis—the Builder. These customers visited retail stores or the company Web site every few months to buy a new piece of gear. They built large systems one component at a time as their finances allowed. Customers who bought everything all at once stood out and easily attracted the company's attention, but the more modest behavior of the Builder allowed them to fly below the radar until the database revealed their existence, their surprising number, and their superior value.

Once they knew about the Builder, CSW quickly shifted its focus. Instead of sales promotions, it provided educational programs designed to build the Builder. These online classes met the customers' need for information and increased the frequency of their visits. Now, as prospects learn about new technologies like high-definition TV, they often decide to buy a new piece of related equipment. By saving the coals and analyzing the data, CSW has found a way to serve its customers and the sales naturally followed.

Who are your most profitable customers? What kinds of promotions will they respond to? Segment your database, study lifetime value figures, and find out.

DEVELOP SEPARATE MARKETING PLANS FOR EACH SEGMENT

Since all customers are not equal, you should not treat them equally with your marketing. Identifying various customer segments allows you to develop marketing strategies optimized for each. Suppose, for instance, you segmented your customers according to their lifetime value. You might find that a small percentage were your highest performers. They bought from you frequently and consistently spent more than others. You might also identify a low-performing group that absorbed repeated marketing campaigns but almost never bought. Their lackluster behavior meant marketing to them never yielded a positive return on your investment. In between lay several other groups of varying value. Using their LTV you could divide your entire customer database into five groups. It might look something like this:

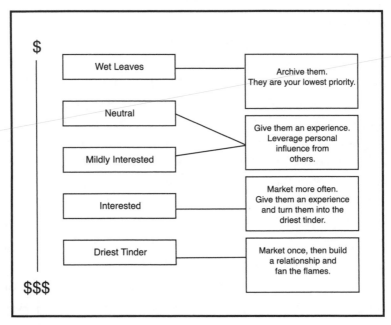

Figure 6.1 Segmenting customers by lifetime value and developing a different approach for each group.

There is more to segmenting customers than their lifetime value. You might try segmenting them by a number of criteria, including their loyalty. In his book *The Loyalty Effect*, Frederick Reichheld identified what he called the loyalty coefficient after noticing that some customers are far more loyal than others. Not coincidentally, the most loyal customers quite often have the highest lifetime value too. By keeping records of both loyal customers and those who leave, you can begin to profile each type. Once you identify the characteristics that define loyal customers, you can develop strategies that attract more of them in the first place.

Try segmenting your customers according to their recommendation behavior too. This characteristic can be a hidden gold mine. Once you identify your most active customer evangelists, you can reward their behavior and equip them for even greater influence. Leveraging these energetic people can dramatically increase your acquisition rates, revenues, and profits. What's more, research shows that referred people are more loyal and spend more than the new acquisitions you find through your marketing efforts.[10]

COLLECT AND CONNECT

Database programs and powerful computers revolutionized marketing. The Internet brought changes even more profound. Together they form a match made in marketing heaven, a one-two punch that allows you to collect reams of valuable consumer data with less effort and expense than ever before and then to use it to better connect with your customers in three important ways: connecting customers to your business, connecting your business to its customers, and connecting your customers to each other. Let's explore them one at a time.

Connecting Customers to Your Business

Connecting customers to your business is about access—theirs, not yours. Remember, PyroMarketing focuses on the consumer, not the company, so let's begin by looking at what your Web site and database can do for your customer.

The Internet simultaneously creates both a problem and an opportunity for businesses like yours. The problem is that the Web makes it easy for customers to learn about your competitors and their products. Consumers are informed as never before and they use that information to make purchase decisions. Unfortunately, knowing more about your competitor's product may lead them to choose it, even if it isn't superior to yours. Your product may have more features or superior performance stats, but if the consumer doesn't know about them, it's as if they don't exist. Fortunately, the Internet can correct the very problem it created.

Use your Web site and database to give consumers virtually unfettered access to your company and its data. Sign them up as members, give them passwords, and let them help themselves. Make it easy for customers to find what they're looking for and you will make an easier sale. In fact, you can even let them ring up the sale. That's what Amazon.com, UPS, and other savvy Web retailers do. It's the online equivalent of letting the customer behind the counter and it meets customer needs while saving you money.

Connecting Your Business to Its Customers

Connecting your business to its customers is all about permission. Can you send them an e-mail newsletter? Of course you can. Should you? Well, that depends on whether you have their permission. Tactics intended to connect your business to its consumers can just as quickly drive them away if you haven't asked for and received their permission.

Connecting your company to your customers is important, but you have got to do it right. First, target the right people. If you're talking to the driest tinder, then you have found a receptive audience. Next, offer them something valuable. Give them information, or greater access, or special offers, or special products, recognition, or rewards. Ask your customers what they want from you besides your product or service and then deliver it. "Database marketing and the web are ways of making customers happy," says Arthur M. Hughes. "[It is a way] of providing them with recognition, service, friendship, and information for which, in return, they will reward you with loyalty, retention and increased sales."[11] So go ahead, make your customers happy. Reach out to them as much as you can with personalized newsletters and e-mail, so long as you have their permission. Use cookies to recognize them each time they return to your site, but only if you have their permission. Whenever you contact your customer, give them permission to leave by making it easy for them to unsubscribe. There is no quicker way to measure the relevance, value, and timeliness of your marketing messages and no better way to keep a marketer on the straight and narrow.

Connecting Customers to Each Other

Connecting customers to each other is all about community. Police are quick to disperse crowds because they understand that the power of a group far exceeds the strength of the individuals that comprise it. Through radiative feedback the members of a gathering are influenced by their network neighbors, increasing their loyalty, certainty, and resolve. They feel part of something bigger than themselves and are encouraged by an aura of invincibility. This can be dangerous when the crowd is contemplating a riot, but a tremendous advantage when they are thinking about buying your product or service.

Your database lists thousands of people who have discovered your company, but are waiting to discover each other. You can improve your business by helping them connect. A 2001 McKinsey-Jupiter Media Metrix study showed that customers of Web community features generate two-thirds of sales despite accounting for only one-third of a site's visitors.[12] "Customers who contribute product reviews or post messages visit community Web sites nine times more often than sites without communities," according to Jackie Huba and Ben McConnell, authors of "Creating Customer Evangelists." "[They] remain twice as loyal, and buy almost twice as often. Even customers who read but don't contribute to community interaction are more frequent visitors and buyers."[13] You can harness that disproportionate influence by building places—virtual and otherwise—where you customers can congregate. Follow the lead set by these forward-thinking companies.

- *Fast Company* magazine created its Company of Friends, a global network of its readers. Members can network with other *Fast Company* readers online and at live events from Seattle to Paris. A search function on its Web site lets you locate groups or even individual members. *Fast Company* connected its readers and is reaping the rewards.
- Barnes and Noble uses its www.bn.com Web site to organize communities of readers into book clubs around a variety of topics, including African American interests, biography, fiction and literature, love and romance, science fiction and fantasy, or by a favorite author. Barnes and Noble even supplies printable reading group guides and a place for the group to meet either online or in their stores.
- Their family lives in more than 100 countries. Their home is any road, any city and any place they choose to gather.

They are the Harley Owners Group (HOG). Started in 1983, HOG has grown into the largest factory-sponsored motorcycle club in the world with more than 900,000 members and 1,350 chapters worldwide. Members can attend rallies and events, receive magazines like *Hog Tales* and *Enthusiast*, join a local chapter, access a special members' Web site and, most important, gather with 900,000 others who share their passion for "making the Harley Davidson Dream a way of life."[14]

Look for ways to connect your customers to each other by creating vibrant customer communities. Create owners groups or online customer support centers where your customers can help each other. Allow your customers to post their profile and connect with other customers. Create a special Web site for fans. Create an e-mail discussion group. The list is endless, but the point is this: don't let your best customers exist in isolation. Connect them to each other and watch your business improve. It's one of the great benefits of saving the coals.

TRUST AND LIFETIME VALUE

Every transaction in a free market economy is a voluntary exchange in which both parties make a profit. In fact, the only reason people or businesses undertake the exchange at all is because they expect a profit. By profit I mean that each party values what they acquire in the transaction more than what they gave up. What's more, whether the parties repeat the exchange in the future depends on whether they got the benefit they were expecting. If consumers consistently profit, they will continue doing business with your company. If they don't, then they will stop. A consumer's value, therefore, is roughly equivalent to their trust. To maximize a consumer's lifetime value, you must maximize the benefit they derive from each transaction, thereby increasing their trust that all future transactions will deliver a profit. The mildly startling consequence of this is that your most profitable customers are the people who consistently profit from doing business with your company. The key to maximizing your company's profits, therefore, is to first maximize your customer's profits. Lifetime value measures more than each customer's value to your company; it also indicates your company's value to each customer.

This is how you keep customers for life. With the help of your database and a trusting relationship, you can collect your customers' information, connect with their passions, interests, and preferred way of doing business, and connect them with each other. If you serve them, then your business, your products, and your services can be their most profitable and you will win your customers' loyalty for life.

CHAPTER SUMMARY

PyroMarketing is about more than starting a fire; it also requires that you preserve it. Keeping a record of your customers in a database helps your marketing build equity, allowing you to spend your next match building a second fire. Build a database to record your customers' demographic and behavioral information. Build ways of capturing this data into every promotion and business process that touches the consumer. Calculate your customers' lifetime value. Segment your customers by a variety of criteria to identify the most profitable, loyal, and enthusiastic. Develop a different marketing strategy for each segment, fanning the flames of the best customers, improving the quality of moderate customers, and archiving the worst. Collect and connect. Once you collect your customers' data, use it to connect them to your business, to connect your business to them, and to connect them to each other. By saving the coals you can start new fires whenever the need arises and do it without new matches.

FLASHPOINTS

1. Are your current marketing efforts focused solely on customer acquisition or are you also taking steps to retain those customers?
2. What consumer information does your company currently have? Where is it stored? Make a list. Then build a single, central database where you can keep all of the consumer data you collect.
3. How can you build ways of collecting consumer data into every marketing promotion?
4. What is your customers' lifetime value? Make your own LTV table and do the calculations.
5. Who are your most valuable customers? What characteristics define them? What marketing strategies will serve them best?
6. Now that you've collected your customers' data, how can you
   a. Connect them to your company?
   b. Connect your company to them?
   c. Connect them to each other?

7

Afterglow

First they ignore you, then they laugh at you,
then they fight you, then you win.
—Mahatma Gandhi

In *A Voice from the Attic,* essayist Robertson Davies said: "The world is full of people whose notion of a satisfactory future is, in fact, a return to the idealized past." So is your office. Without knowing it, Davies was describing many of the people you will encounter as you shift your approach from mass marketing to PyroMarketing. Now that you understand the driest tinder's susceptibility to your marketing message, the ability of experience to sway people's choices, the power of personal persuasion to expand the reach of your marketing, and the equity-building wisdom of saving the coals, do you really want to rely on the same old mass marketing tactics? How could you? In a crowded marketplace drowning in a tide of advertising babble, you need a way to survive on a single match in the frozen wilderness. Most of the people with whom you work will not get it. They will long for the idealized past and resist your attempts to lead your organization down this new path.

At first they will ignore you, then they will laugh at you ("Wait, wait, let me get this straight . . . you plan to sell more by concentrating on fewer people? . . . ha, ha, ha!"), and as you begin to make progress, they may even fight you. Don't despair. If you persevere then you will win—and so will your company.

Over the last several chapters we have looked closely at the evidence behind PyroMarketing. We have studied the psychological, physiological, and sociological reasons for each step. Now it's time to change our perspective, to step back a bit, and see how the pieces of PyroMarketing fit together into a cohesive, comprehensive, repeatable marketing strategy and how companies are already using and benefiting from its principles. Some of these examples may help you convince the doubters.

THE PURPOSE-DRIVEN® LIFE

Every book aspires to be a bestseller, but very few achieve it. Not only was *The Purpose-Driven® Life* a bestseller, its success was unprecedented. *Publishers Weekly* declared it "the best-selling hardback in American history." How did this one book accomplish what millions more fail to attain? Its success was a side effect of a ministry campaign that, perhaps unknowingly, modeled the four steps that define PyroMarketing.

To launch the Forty Days of Purpose Campaign, Rick Warren began with the driest tinder. Since the early 1990s he had been serving thousands of pastors across the country and around the world with his www.pastors.com Web site. Member pastors could download sermons, teaching tools, and other aids that helped them serve their church more easily. Many of these pastors had read his book *The Purpose-Driven® Church* and successfully applied its principles. They had experienced success with Warren's programs before. He had proven himself to these people, winning their trust and admiration.

When it was time to launch the Forty Days of Purpose Campaign, he sent a message to the pastors on his list and twelve hundred signed on.

Every aspect of the six-week campaign touched people with the match. They read the book each day, they listened to sermons each Sunday, and they met with friends each week to discuss the book's content. By the campaign's end, four hundred thousand people were intimately familiar with the book and its many benefits. They knew its message, but more important, they had firsthand experience of its power to change a life. They were not just readers; they were an unstoppable army of customer evangelists ready to sing the book's praises to all who would listen.

The campaign fanned the flames, too. The book explained God's five purposes for a person's life and the final purpose was evangelism. At the end of the campaign, just as they reached the zenith of their experience, people were told to share the gospel message with others. The book, the sermons, and the small groups focused on the same message. "This is too good to keep to ourselves. We have got to tell others." And so they did. The campaign did little more than make the suggestion that people spread the word, but that was all it took. As people told their friends about Jesus, they would often mention *The Purpose-Driven® Life* as a way to learn more. Within four months, four hundred thousand initial book sales had quintupled to two million. From the first campaign and for the next couple of years, it seemed that for every book sold at a discount to someone in a church-based campaign, five more books were sold through retail stores. Fanning the flames didn't just double the campaign's impact; it multiplied it by a factor of five!

Not only did people recommend the book, pastors told other pastors to try the campaign. A large percentage of the five thousand–plus churches in the fall 2004 campaign signed up at the recommendation of another pastor.

Finally, the Forty Days of Purpose Campaign saved the coals by keeping a record of the churches that participated in the campaign and the people who read the book. By signing up at www.purposedrivenlife.com, individuals could give a testimony of how the book had changed their life, and many have. Another database records the twenty thousand–plus churches that hosted a campaign.

THE PASSION OF THE CHRIST

The Passion of the Christ didn't stand a chance. Mel Gibson and his Icon Productions company were ostracized by many of the same Hollywood insiders that most films depend upon for their success. Reviewers lambasted the film as too violent or anti-Semitic. Distributors avoided it like . . . like . . . like a movie about Jesus, and refused to supply the $30 million for marketing that has become the average for a major motion picture. Without a marketing war chest Gibson couldn't use the mass advertising tactics available to other films. It's no surprise then that his movie made only . . . no, that can't be right . . . over $500 million! "Most films don't break even with just domestic distribution." according to BoxOfficeMojo.com president Brandon Gray. "Normally they need international box office, and rental and sales income from DVDs and video [to do that]."[1] Yet by just the fifth day in domestic theaters, *The Passion of the Christ* had earned $125 million in box office

receipts against only about $45 million in combined market-
ing and production costs.

Mel Gibson couldn't return to the idealized past because
he couldn't afford to. He had no choice but press ahead with
less expensive PyroMarketing, and boy did it work. He began
by gathering the driest tinder and touching it with the match.
In private screenings Gibson showed his film to six or eight
pastors at a time. Then he would fan the flames by leveraging
their positive experience to woo six or eight more. As word of
his film spread through the affiliation network of pastors, the
crowds at his screenings grew until, a couple of months
before the film's release, he was screening it for five thousand
pastors in mega–church auditoriums.

He fanned the flames by equipping pastors with tools for
spreading word of the movie to the people in their church.
Ordinarily you would see movie trailers on television or
before other films in the theater, but millions of people saw
the trailer for *The Passion of the Christ* in their church. Icon
Productions supplied movie trailers to pastors who enthusiastically played them for their congregation on Sunday morning. An organization called Outreach Marketing set up a Web
site with resources for churches, including thirteen ideas on
how they could use the film, outlines for complimentary sermons, and suggestions for establishing discussion groups.
They produced *Passion*-themed invitation cards, evangelistic
booklets, bulletin inserts, and even doorknob hangers that
could be personalized to invite the community to specific
local churches.[2]

The Mountaintop Church in Vestavia Hills, Alabama,
exemplified many churches when it bought all the tickets to
two Saturday matinees of *The Passion of the Christ* and
offered free tickets to each parishioner who would bring a

nonchurchgoer to see the movie.[3] "A lot of church leaders . . . went out and told their congregations to see the film—they actually booked tickets themselves," said Greg Kilday of *The Hollywood Reporter*. "Some theaters have . . . sold out their opening days to church affiliated groups, so we really haven't seen this kind of grass roots campaign take off like this before."[4]

Astoundingly, more than four hundred pastors paid $795 each for a television commercial featuring clips from the film before paying even more to place it on their local television station. They were not merely spreading word of mouth; these customer evangelists were spending their money to help market the movie![5]

The Web site www.storiesofthepassion.com fanned the flames even further by allowing people to reach beyond their social network and tell complete strangers about their experience with the film. Not only did this site fan the flames, it saved the coals too by collecting each person's name, address, city, state, zip, e-mail address, Web site, and personal testimony regarding the film. It also respected their privacy and built trust by asking for permission to send additional messages.

The "Student Mobilizer" at www.studentshavepassion.com equipped college students with a variety of tools for spreading word of the film, including flyers, free ads, bulletins, fax blasts, and html e-mail messages. It included an area for buying tickets and a group e-mail message featuring the movie trailer you could use to invite all your friends. Student Mobilizer forums let customer evangelists talk about the film online with other like-minded people.

These PyroMarketing tactics were unusual for a movie and delivered surprising results from unexpected places. *The Passion* opened on 4,643 screens in 3,006 theaters; however the top markets were Greenwood, Meridian, Hattiesburg-Laurel, and Jackson, all in Mississippi; and Abilene-Sweetwater, Texas. Those markets don't align with either the top traditional theatrical markets or the top markets for DVD sales. But they did deliver the top-grossing R-rated movie of all time.

First they ignored Mel Gibson, then they laughed at him, then they fought him, then he won.

JESUS OF NAZARETH

If the success of *The Passion of the Christ* seems unlikely, then the growth and endurance of Christianity over the last two thousand years is nothing short of miraculous. Founded by an itinerant Jewish carpenter before the invention of the word "marketing" or the tools it typically employs, and despite homicidal persecution throughout the centuries, it has prospered to become the world's largest religion. Globally, more than two billion people call themselves Christians, but as with all such phenomena, it started small and then it grew.

Though he eventually preached to crowds of five thousand, Jesus began his ministry with the driest tinder by calling just twelve disciples. These men were so inclined toward his message that they left their jobs, families, and possessions after a single exposure to that message. Next, he touched them with the match by giving them an experience with his power. Jesus didn't boast that he was the son of God; in fact, he admitted it only reluctantly. Instead, he healed the lame and restored sight to the blind and fed multitudes from a single sack lunch. Much more than words, these experiences convinced the disciples of his divinity. "Who do you say that I am?" Jesus asked Peter "You are the Christ of God," Peter replied.[6]

Though the church found its beginning in Jesus, the disciples were responsible for its growth. Following his Resurrection and before his Ascension, Jesus gave his disciples the great commission. "Go into all the world and preach the good news to all creation,"[7] Jesus commanded. But he didn't just tell the disciples to spread his message, he equipped them for success by fanning the flames. "But you will receive power when the Holy Spirit comes on you; and you will be my witnesses in Jerusalem, and in all Judea and Samaria, and to the ends of the earth."[8]

Properly equipped the disciples were an unstoppable force. They walked to the ends of the earth as Jesus commanded and shared the good news despite brutal persecution. Most died as martyrs spreading a message that was not originally their own. Their work built the early Christian church; it was an eager fire that spread throughout the world.

Finally, Jesus saved the coals. He has a record of every individual and their deeds from all human history called the Book of Life. Yes, Jesus has a consumer database and no, you can't rent his list.

ONSTAR

Some businesses use select PyroMarketing principles successfully, even though they have yet to assemble them all into a comprehensive campaign. General Motors' OnStar division touches people with the match with its service and its advertising.

OnStar isn't easy to explain and that could make it difficult to advertise. It is a communications system built into select General Motors' cars and trucks. By pressing a button in the roof console you are connected via satellite with an OnStar adviser and can speak with them using a built-in hands-free speakerphone. The adviser provides a variety of safety and convenience services to people who subscribe and pay a monthly fee. If your air bag deploys, for example, the vehicle sends a signal to an OnStar adviser who will try calling you in the car. If you don't respond, then they assume the worst, call the police, and, using tracking data from the satellites, tell them your vehicle's location. By communicating with the vehicle's engine control computer they can remotely diagnose a problem. Using similar technology they will remotely unlock your doors if you've locked the keys inside or track the car if it's stolen. When you are away from your car, you can call them from your cell phone and with a signal bounced off orbiting satellites they will flash your car lights and honk its horn if, for example, you've lost it in the mall parking lot.

Rather than trying to explain such a complicated service, OnStar touches people with a match. When you buy a vehicle equipped with OnStar technology, you get the first year of service free. Very soon, people who couldn't imagine how they would use the service can't imagine living without it.

In its radio advertising OnStar touches people with the match by playing clips from real, live interactions between subscribers and OnStar advisers. When you hear the initial panic in the voice of the woman who locked her keys—and her infant son—in the car, you begin to imagine your own anguish in that situation. When you hear the baby's burbles and the mother's sobs of joy as the command from the OnStar satellite reunites the family by unlocking the car doors, you imagine yourself experiencing that same joy.

What if OnStar also fanned the flames? What if they leveraged the influence of their existing subscribers to promote the service to their friends? How much more successful might they be? OnStar could award its subscribers points every time they let a friend try the service by pressing the button in their car to get a restaurant recommendation from the OnStar adviser. Subscribers could save points and exchange them for prizes, or perhaps discounts, on new GM cars.

AMERICA ONLINE

America Online is another company that practices an incomplete form of PyroMarketing. Nevertheless, the portions they use work quite well.

The other day I received an AOL CD in the mail. By placing it in my computer, I could try many hours of their service at no cost. This is a great example of touching people with the match and AOL rode this one PyroMarketing principle to dominance as an Internet service provider. Unlike dozens of AOL CDs I had received before, this one also fanned the flames. Instead of a single user-name and password, this CD came with two. After using the first to try the service myself, I was supposed to give the CD to a friend, allowing them to use the other. AOL was fanning the flames by leveraging each recipient to reach one more and, in the process, doubling the reach of its demo discs.

AOL needs to work on saving the coals, however. The disc I received was addressed to "Resident at ———" and listed my street address. If they had checked the mailing list for that promotion against their existing customer database they would have discovered that I already subscribed.

AMAZON.COM

Amazon.com employs several PyroMarketing principles in its service. Its "Look Inside the Book" feature touches people with the match by letting them explore a book online the way they would in a brick-and-mortar bookstore.

They fan the flames in several ways. By allowing me to post reviews, they give me a chance to influence other people's book purchases. Some people post negative reviews, but most of the people who take the time to write do so because they loved the book.

By showing me the books purchased by people who also bought the one I'm considering, they use the power of social proof to influence additional purchases. Their many best-sellers lists and the Amazon.com ranking accomplish the same thing.

Amazon's affiliate program is another example of fanning the flames. By promoting titles on their own Web site and linking them back to Amazon, affiliates can earn a small com-mission whenever a customer referred by their site buys a book. Amazon.com fans the flames with its affiliate program by enlisting ordinary citizens to, in effect, open Amazon.com branches all over the World Wide Web.

Amazon.com is also adept at saving the coals. They keep robust customer profiles and know how to use them. A friend of mine once received an e-mail from Amazon.com. They had analyzed his purchase behavior and, based on their findings, were recommending ten new books they thought he might like. Amazingly, their profile was so accurate that my friend already owned six of the ten books they recommended.

VOLVO

Some companies don't use PyroMarketing, but they should. In 1994, Volvo's advertising agency convinced it to spend $2.65 million—more than a third of its annual budget—to advertise its semi-tractors on television during the Super Bowl.[9] The ad was designed to appeal to truck drivers and demonstrate the truck's comfort and luxury. Volvo hoped truck drivers would influence the executives who decided which trucks to buy for their fleet. The plan was expensive and hopelessly indirect. A classic example of trying to sell a niche product with mass marketing methods, it was fraught with problems.

First, by Volvo's own admission, only about 1 percent of the Super Bowl viewing audience had any affiliation whatsoever with the trucking industry. Beyond wasting its advertising on over 140 million people who had no interest in or need for their product, Volvo had other problems. Only a small percentage of that 1 percent would notice its brief ad. An even smaller group would be influenced by it because truckers can be fiercely brand loyal. They are "Peterbilt Guys" or "Mack Men" and often disdain competing brands. Even supposing some tiny percentage was influenced, the strategy assumed that those drivers had access to the executives who specify the fleet, but most often they don't. Even if the ad convinced a driver to try a Volvo, there was almost nothing he could do about it since the truck was specified by someone he didn't know or have any contact with.

But suppose they did. Suppose a handful of the drivers who were influenced by the ad actually spoke with the fleet manager and said, "You really ought to think about buying Volvos for the fleet instead of whatever truck you've been buying. I saw their ad in the Super Bowl and they looked pretty nice." The plan assumed the driver's comments would somehow make a difference. Unfortunately for Volvo, the features that motivate drivers often don't matter as much to fleet managers. Drivers care about comfort. Fleet managers care about costs. Fleet managers wonder how a Volvo's maintenance costs compare with those of other brands. How much do they cost per mile to operate? Will I have to retrain my mechanics to understand a new and different kind of truck? Will I need to invest in a new and expensive parts inventory? What kind of service and support can I expect from the manufacturer? How do Volvos hold their value compared with other trucks? Whether the driver feels cool and comfortable in the truck is not as high on their list of priorities.

Using a mass marketing strategy, Volvo advertised a message that didn't matter to people who couldn't buy their product. Pyro-Marketing would have approached Volvo's challenge differently.

There are two kinds of truckers: private carriers whose fleets haul their own products and common carriers who haul other companies' goods. Two trade associations organize and support the two groups. They are the National Private Truck Council and the American Trucking Association. Their combined membership totals just 2,900 and comprises the decision makers for truck purchases. Volvo didn't need to reach hundreds of millions of people with its advertising; it needed to reach just 2,900—the driest tinder. By refocusing the $2.65 million it spent on an ad during the Super Bowl on the driest tinder instead, Volvo would have had $913 for each of the 2,900 who buy almost every semi-tractor in the United States—enough money to try something very different.

Instead of trying to indirectly communicate with this group by way of a couple of fleeting television commercials relayed by drivers, Volvo could have touched them directly with the match. Using the money it spent on the Super Bowl advertising, Volvo could have flown each of the 2,900 decision makers to its headquarters in Greensboro, North Carolina. It could have picked them up at the airport in one of the trucks and, because many fleet managers also have their commercial driver's license, let them drive the truck back to Volvo's offices. While in town, each person could take a tour of the facility, meet Volvo employees, go through a series of educational sessions designed to answer their questions about costs and maintenance. They could take them out for dinner that night (driving the truck, of course), put them up in a hotel, treat them to breakfast and lunch the next day and still have enough left over to give them a Volvo shirt or hat as a parting gift. Which approach do you think would have the most influence on the people who actually sign purchase orders for new trucks? Which would sell trucks and create customer evangelists?

Volvo could have fanned the flames by bringing people to its offices in groups of ten or twelve. By making sure that some of its most loyal customers were mixed into every group, Volvo would create vulnerable clusters and leverage the customer evangelists to influence their peers. By recording each person's experience with digital photos sent to them by e-mail when they returned home, Volvo would have fanned the flames even further by helping each visitor tell others about their experience. And by keeping a database of those who attend, they would save the coals, making it possible to send follow-up correspondence, or invite them to future events.

ALTERNATE ENDINGS

If I asked you to make an inventory of marketing tactics, you would probably list things like magazine ads, newspaper ads, television ads, trade show booths, radio advertising, direct mail pieces, brochures, or ink pens bearing your company name. You might even list Super Bowl ads. Those are the tactics people associate with marketing. Because they go by the name advertising, we often believe that name guarantees results. It doesn't.

I'm quite sure your list would not include airline flights, rides in trucks, or equipment maintenance training sessions as marketing tactics, but for Volvo that is exactly what they could have been.

Albert Einstein defined insanity as "doing the same thing over and over again and expecting different results."[10] For years you have been trained to think like a mass marketer, but that thinking will keep leading you to the same tactics and the same disappointing results. Volvo thought like a mass marketer and ended up with ads for heavy trucks during the Super Bowl while missing an approach that could have made a significant difference. That's insane.

If you want to change how your story ends, you must change the way you think. Forget what you know about marketing. Begin each campaign with a blank sheet of paper and four questions: Who is the driest tinder for my product? How can I touch them with the match? How can I fan the flames? What opportunities do I have to save the coals? If you think hard and answer honestly, then your plans will include marketing tactics that you never before considered but will deliver results you never dreamt were possible. By adopting a new approach to starting a fire in the wilderness, your one match has the power to change the way your story ends.

TO BUILD A FIRE

The *Century* magazine published Jack London's famous short story "To Build a Fire," in August of 1908. It is the version people know, if they know the story at all, but it is not the only one London wrote. He wrote another, juvenile account.[11] The two stories were similar in many ways except that this juvenile version was shorter and in it the Man had a name.

Tom Vincent was traveling alone through the wilderness on a bleak January day, following Paul Creek on his way to Calumet Camp in temperatures of sixty degrees below zero and falling. Halfway to his destination he paused for lunch, but quickly chilled as he stood to eat his biscuits and bacon and returned to jogging up the trail to restore his warmth before finishing his meal. Chilling so quickly was a new experience for him. This was, undoubtedly, the coldest snap he had ever experienced.

Despite the cold Tom Vincent was self-assured—even cocky. London wrote: "He was doing something, achieving something, mastering the elements. Once he laughed aloud in sheer strength of life, and with his clenched fist defied the frost. He was its master. What he did he did in spite of it. It could not stop him. He was going on to the Cherry Creek Divide.

"Strong as were the elements, he was stronger. At such times animals crawled away into their holes and remained in hiding. But he did not hide. He was out in it, facing it, fighting it. He was a man, a master of things."

The wilderness, though, was determined to humble Tom Vincent as it would humble the Man. Paul Creek was frozen solid but from the mountain's side ran several springs whose waters would pool atop the frozen creek to a depth of eight to twelve inches before the top would freeze in a thin layer of ice. The process repeated itself; pooling and freezing, pooling and freezing in layers topped with about an inch of recent snow to "make the trap complete."

Tom Vincent did not see the danger, but felt it quickly enough as toward the middle of the pool he broke through and the icy waters bit at his feet and ankles. He lunged toward the bank, reaching it in half a dozen awkward steps. "He was quite cool and collected. The thing to do, and the only thing to do, was to build a fire," wrote London. "He knew, further, that great care must be exercised; that with failure at the first attempt, the chance was made greater for failure at the second attempt. In short, he knew that there must be no failure.

The moment before a strong, exulting man, boastful of his mastery of the elements, he was now fighting for his life against those same elements."[11]

He scrambled up the bank and gathered material for his fire. He removed his mittens and reached into his coat, pulling birch bark and a bundle of matches from its inside pocket. He struck a match and built his fire. The fire was young but growing and he was adding the first large sticks when the snow from the pine boughs overhead descended upon Tom Vincent and his fire. Startled and afraid, he stepped back from beneath the pine tree and tried to build another fire. By now his fingers were stiff and numb from the cold. With great difficulty he separated a new match from the bundle and tried to light it but dropped it into the snow and could not pick it up again.

Now he was desperate. He stood and beat his mittened hands against the tree trunk to restore circulation, warmth, and feeling to his hands. He recovered enough to light a second match and the remaining piece of birch bark, but he was cold and shivering and quenched the tiny flame as he clumsily tried adding twigs. His fire was out and Tom Vincent sank down into the snow, sobbing, and certain he would die.

The two versions of Jack London's story are nearly identical except for their length, the man's name, and what happens next. Tom Vincent lives! I'll let London tell it from here.

But the love of life was strong in him, and he sprang again to his feet. He was thinking quickly. What if the matches did burn his hands? Burned hands were better than dead hands. No hands at all were better than death. He floundered along the trail until be came upon another high-water lodgment. There were twigs and branches, leaves and grasses, all dry and waiting the fire. [Dry tinder!]

Again he sat down and shuffled the bunch of matches on his knees, got it into place on his palm, with the wrist of his other hand forced the nerveless fingers down against the bunch, and with the wrist kept them there. At the second scratch the bunch caught fire, and he knew that if he could stand the pain he was saved. He choked with the sulphur fumes, and the blue flame licked the flesh of his hands.

At first he could not feel it, but it burned quickly in through the frosted surface. The odor of the burning flesh—his flesh—was strong in his nostrils. He writhed about in his torment, yet held on. He set his teeth and swayed back and forth, until the clear white flame of the burning match shot up, and he had applied that flame to the leaves and grasses. [Touch it with the match!]

An anxious five minutes followed, but the fire gained steadily. Then he set to work to save himself. Heroic measures were necessary, such was his extremity, and he took them.

Alternately rubbing his hands with snow and thrusting them into the flames, and now and again beating them against the hard trees, he restored their circulation sufficiently for them to be of use to him. With his hunting-knife he slashed the straps from his pack, unrolled his blanket, and got out dry socks and footgear.

Then be cut away his moccasins and bared his feet. But while he had taken liberties with his hands, he kept his feet fairly away from the fire and rubbed them with snow. He rubbed till his hands grew numb, when he would cover his feet with the blanket, warm his hands by the fire, and return to the rubbing.

For three hours he worked, till the worst effects of the freezing had been counteracted. All that night he stayed by the fire, and it was late the next day when be limped pitifully into the camp on the Cherry Creek Divide.

In a month's time he was able to be about on his feet, although the toes were destined always after that to be very sensitive to frost. But the scars on his hands he knows he will carry to the grave. And—*"Never travel alone!"* he now lays down the precept of the North.

For PyroMarketers there is an alternate fate. You may be alone in the freezing wilderness with only one match, but it will not stop you. Though the elements are strong, you can be stronger. By gathering the driest tinder, touching it with the match, fanning the flames and saving the coals, you can master the wilderness—defy the frost—and build a lifesaving fire.

PyroMarketing Plan

Now that you understand PyroMarketing, it's time to begin using it. The following questions will lead you to a PyroMarketing plan for your product or service. This is simply a starting point. Feel free to modify it to better fit your business. An electronic version in template form, along with other PyroMarketing tools, is available online at www.pyromarketing.com.

PRODUCT/SERVICE DESCRIPTION

1. Write a description of the product/service being promoted. Write it from your perspective.
2. Write a description of the product/service being promoted, but write it from the consumer's perspective. Be sure to include any skepticism they may feel. Is this description different from the company perspective?
3. Write a one-sentence description of the product/service from the consumer's perspective. If you can't describe it with one sentence, you may have a problem. This sentence is the one that people will use when telling others about your product/service. If you can't describe it in one sentence, then your customers may have trouble too and that

could inhibit your fire. If you can't improve your description, maybe you need to improve your product/service.

4. What benefit will people enjoy by using your product/service? Be honest. Don't exaggerate.

Driest Tinder

To get the most out of PyroMarketing you must be ruthless when defining the driest tinder. Define a group most likely to buy, then ask which of that group are even more likely, then ask again, then drill down further, then prioritize them again. Think of the Olympic trials for a track event. Hundreds of the country's best athletes run in the early heats. Each of them is extremely fast but the vast majority won't make it because they aren't the *fastest*. In heat after heat the slower runners are eliminated and the fastest move on until two or three are chosen to represent their country at the games.

Dry is not good enough. You want the driest. Be honest. Be ruthless. And be confident that even a narrowly defined group is still quite large. This is the point of origin for your fire. Begin it with the driest and their bright, hot flame will quickly expand the blaze beyond this initial group.

1. Describe the kind of person who is most likely to buy. These people are the dry tinder.

2. Picture a group of people like you just described. Within that group some people will be even more likely to buy than others. Who are they and why? Forget demographics and define them by their behavior. What do they do? How do they feel? These people are drier tinder.

3. Now, consider the subgroup defined in paragraph 2 above and ask which of the people in that group exhibit the behav-

ior most often? Who feels those feelings the strongest? What traits or behaviors distinguish them from the rest of the group? These people are the driest tinder.

4. Where do the driest tinder organize? Where do they congregate to celebrate their passion, pursue their interest, or find camaraderie with others like themselves? List the places, organizations, etc.

5. What communications channels have these organizations built to support their organization? Conferences? Magazines? Newsletters? Web sites? Search the Internet to see what you can find. Follow the web of links and associations to map out the driest tinder's social network. Make contact with people at those organizations and ask for their help reaching their people.

Touch Them with the Match

1. Where will people use your product/service?
2. When will people use your product/service?
3. How can you allow people to try it in those, or similar, circumstances?
4. Is it possible to give your product to the driest tinder? Might that be less expensive than traditional advertising?

Fan the Flames

1. How can you help people forward your promotional messages? List at least three ways.
2. How can your customers help others experience your product or service? List three ways.

Save the Coals

1. How will this marketing plan collect and record consumer data?
2. How will you use that data to further this plan?

APPENDIX B

www.pyromarketing.com

I encourage you to visit the PyroMarketing Web site. Among its many features, you will find

- A pdf version of the Introduction that you can print and share with your staff
- Information on ways to share PyroMarketing with your company or association with speaking engagements and workshops
- PowerPoint presentations you can use to teach PyroMarketing principles to your company, department, or class
- A number of creative, fun ways to fan the flames for this book
- How to become a member and receive the "PyroMarketing Fire Alarm" newsletter
- Ways to connect with other PyroMarketing readers
- Illustrations of some of the tools used in the PyroMarketing campaigns for *The Purpose-Driven® Life* and *The Passion of the Christ*
- Links to companies that can help you create and implement successful PyroMarketing campaigns
- Ways to connect and interact with me

Notes

INTRODUCTION

1 Jennifer Reingold, "How to Read a Business Book," *Fast Company*, November 2004, p.106.

2 http://www.chicagohs.org/fire/conflag/ (April 18, 2005).

3 http://www.censusscope.org/us/m1600/chart_popl.html (April 18, 2005).

4 http://www.chicagohs.org/fire/witnesses/ (April 18, 2005).

CHAPTER 1: FROM FLOODS TO FLAMES

1 Bill Kelley and Hugh Wilson, *Blast from the Past*, http://www.allmoviescripts.com/scripts/13979971303f331811a6086.html (April 18, 2005).

2 "Brand Journalism?" www.sethgodin.com, November 30, 2004.

3 "Marketing in the New Millennium," http://www.sba.gov/gopher/Business-Development/Success-series/Vol8/mrkting.txt (April 18, 2005).

4 Anthony Bianco, "The Vanishing Mass Market," *BusinessWeek*, July 12, 2004, p 61.

5 Al Ries and Laura Ries, *The Fall of Advertising and the Rise of PR*. (New York: HarperBusiness, 2002), p. 63.

6 http://www.nielsenmedia.com/newsreleases/2002/2002%20 Pre-Super%20Bowl.htm (March 5, 2005).

7 "Some 'Dot-Coms' Fumble Efforts to Score in Ad Game," www.latimes.com:80/business/20000131/t000009800.html.

8 Gwendolyn Mariano, "Super Bowl Ads return to offline giants," February 1, 2002, http://news.com.com/2100-1023-828135.html.

9 Ries and Ries, *The Fall of Advertising*, p.65.

10 Daniel J. Boorstin, *The Americans: The Democratic Experience*. (New York: Vintage Books, 1974), p. 101.

11 Ibid.

12 Richard Digby-Junger, "Mass Market Magazine Revolution," http://www.findarticles.com/p/articles/mi_gleps/is_tov/ai_2419100778/print (April 18, 2005).

13 Digby-Junger.

14 http://www.factmonster.com/ipka/A0151956.html (March 7, 2005).

15 Boorstin, p. 392.

16 Ibid., p. 393.

17 Bianco, p. 62.

18 Boorstin, p. 391.

19 Ibid., p. 146.

20 Ibid., p. 263.

21 Digby-Junger.

22 Boorstin, p. 307.

23 Joseph Wilke, "The Future of Simulated Test Markets: The Coming Obsolescence of Current Models and the Characteristics of Models of the Future," http://www.bases.com/news/news%20092002.html (March 7, 2005).

24 Quoted in Boorstin, p. ix.

25 Bianco, p. 67.

26 David Brooks, "Take a Ride to Exubria," *New York Times*, November 9, 2004.

27 Boorstin, p. 269.

28 William Gargan, "The Demassification of Media," http://www.wgaprc.com /guests/dthoads.html (April 18, 2005).

29 "The Media in the United States," http://www.usinfo.org/usia/usinfo.state .gov/usa/infousa/media/media1cd.htm (April 18, 2005).

30 Albert-Laszlo Barabasi, *Linked*, (New York: Plume, 2003), p. 165.

31 Robert D. Putnam, *Bowling Alone: The Collapse and Revival of American Community*, (New York:Touchstone Books, 2001).

32 Ibid.

33 Bianco, p. 63.

34 Rick Mates, "Cable TV Offerings Put Broadcast Stations in a Bind," http://www.scrantontimes.com (July 13, 2002).

35 Quoted in Putnam, p.224.

36 Ibid.

37 Ibid.

38 Don E. Schultz, Stanley I. Tannenbaum, and Robert F. Lauterborn, *The New Marketing Paradigm*, (Lincolnwood, Illinois: NTC Business Books, 1993), p. 5.

39 http://www.blupete.com/Literature/Biographies/Science/Copernicus.htm (March 14, 2005).

40 Quoted in Cecil Adams, "What's the Story on That Weird Medieval Cult? The Flatulents? Plus, Do the Chinese Use Water Torture?" http://www .straightdope.com/columns/010112.html (January 12, 2001).

41 http://www.captiveaudience.org/arbitron.html (March 7, 2005).

42 Ibid.

43 Ibid.

44 Donald J. Boudreau, "Puffery in Advertising," *The Free Market*, vol. 13, no. 9, September 1995.

45 Malcolm Gladwell, "The Spin Myth," *New Yorker*, July 6, 1998.

46 Quoted in Boorstin, p. ix.

CHAPTER 2: FIRE

1 "How to Read a Business Book," *Fast Company*, November 2004, p. 106.

2 James Surowiecki, "The Decline of Brands," , *Wired*, Issue 12.11, November 2004, http://www.wired.com/wired/archive/12.11/brands.html (March 7, 2005).

3 Ibid.

4 Ed Keller and John Berry, *The Influentials*, (New York: Free Press, 2003), p. 170.

5 Al Ries and Laura Ries, *The Fall of Advertising and the Rise of PR*, (New York: HarperBusiness, 2002), p. 74.

6 Surowiecki.

7 International Fire Service Training Association, *Essentials of Fire Fighting*, 3rd ed. (Stillwater, Oklahoma: 1992), p. 5.

8 For more information about the fire triangle and combustion, see http:// www.firesafe.org.uk/html/miscellaneous/firetria.htm (April 18, 2005).

9 Quoted in "Open Wide," James Surowiecki, The Financial Page, *The New Yorker*, August 4, 2003, http://www.newyorker.com/printable/?talk/030804 ta_talk_surowiecki (November 29, 2004).

10 Ibid.

11 Quoted in ibid.

12 Research study conducted by DDM Marketing Communications for Zondervan and Family Christian Stores in September 2004.

13 "USA Today Top 150," November 29, 2004, http://www.usatoday.com.

14 Seth Godin, *The Purple Cow*, (New York: Portfolio, 2003), p. 121.

15 "Fuels and Ignition Temperatures," http://engineeringtoolbox.com /9_171.html (November 10, 2004).

16 http://yubanet.com/news_releases.shtml (March 7, 2005).

17 Vytenis Babrauskas, "Heat Release Rate: A Brief Primer," http://doctorfire.com/hrr_prmr.html (November 10, 2004).

18 International Fire Service Training Association, p. 5.
19 http://www.usfa.fema.gov/about/media/2003releases/03-120403.shtm (April 18, 2005).
20 International Fire Service Training Association, p. 13.

CHAPTER 3: GATHER THE DRIEST TINDER

1 http://fema.gov/emanagers/2004/nat081504.shtm (April 18, 2005).
2 Matthew 4: 17–20 (NIV).
3 Mary O.Howard, "Selective Perception: An Introduction," http://www.ciadvertising.org/student_account/fall_01/adv382j/howardmo /selectiveperception.html (April 18, 2005).
4 Don E. Schultz, Stanley I. Tannenbaum, and Robert F. Lauterborn, *The New Marketing Paradigm*, (Lincolnwood, Illinois: NTC Business Books, 1993) p. 6.
5 Ibid., p. 26.
6 Quoted in Howard.
7 Elizabeth Bales Frank, "Mysterious Inclinations: The Novels of Shirley Hazzard," http://www.chicklit.com/bundle/bundle25.html (March 7, 2005).
8 Marcia D'Arcangelo, "How Does the Brain Develop?: A Conversation with Steven Petersen," *Educational Leadership*, November 2000, p. 68.
9 Michael D. Lemonick, "Glimpses of the Mind," *Time*, July 17, 1995, pp. 44–52.
10 Ruth Palombo Weiss, "Brain-Based Learning," *Training and Development* vol. 54, no. 7, (July 2000) pp. 20–24.
11 Ibid.
12 Malcolm Gladwell, "Baby Steps: Do Our First Three Years of Life Determine How We'll Turn Out?" *New Yorker*, January 10, 2000.
13 "People's Perceptions of Themselves and Others: Do We Perceive the World Accurately?" http://www.uwm.edu/~hynan/205/205PERCE.html (March 7, 2005).
14 Clive Thompson, "There's a Sucker Born in Every Medial Prefrontal Cortex," *New York Times*, October 26, 2003.
15 Matthew 13:23 (NIV).
16 Matthew 13:9 (NIV).

CHAPTER 4: TOUCH IT WITH THE MATCH

1 Peter M.Leschak, *Ghosts of the Fireground*, (New York: HarperSanFrancisco, 2002), pp. 4, 14.
2 Karl F. Kuhn, Ph.D., *Basic Physics: A Self Teaching Guide*, (New York: Wiley, 1979).

3 Ibid.
4 Linton Weeks, "No Book Report: Skim It and Weep," http://www
.washingtonpost.com/ac2/wp-dyn/A23370-2001May13 (April 18, 2005).
5 W. Huitt, "The Information Processing Approach to Cognition,"
Educational Psychology Interactive, 2003, http://Chiron.valdosta.edu
/whuitt/col/cogsys/infoproc.html (March 7, 2005).
6 Daniel Goleman, *Emotional Intelligence* (New York: Bantam, 1957), p. 6.
7 Ibid., pp. 17–18.
8 Terry Martin, "Global Smoking Statistics for 2002," http://quitsmoking
.about.com/cs/antismoking/a/statistics.htm (October 30, 2004).
9 American Cancer Society, "Guide for Quitting Smoking," http://www
.cancer.org/docrrot/PED/content/PED_10_13X_Quitting_Smoking.asp
(April 18, 2005).
10 Ruth Palombo Weiss, "Emotion and Learning—Implications of New
Neurological Research for Training Techniques," American Society for
Training and Development, Inc. 2000, http://findarticles.com/p/articles
/mi_m4467/is_11_54/ai_67590800 (March 11, 2005).
11 Huitt.
12 Ibid.
13 Joanna Schaffhausen, "The Pleasure Principle: Connections between
Reward and Learning," http://www.brainconnection.com/topics
/?main=fa/pleasure-principle (October 30, 2004).
14 "The Reward Circuit: The Brain from Top to Bottom,"
http://www.thebrain.mcgill.ca/flash/i/i_03/i_03_cl_que/i_03_cl_que.html
(October 30, 2004).
15 "The Reward Circuit: The Brain from Top to Bottom," http://www
.thebrain.mcgill.ca/flash/d/d_03/d_03_cl_que/d_03_cl_que.html
November 2, 2004).
16 "Seeking Pleasure and Avoiding Pain: The Brain from Top to Bottom,"
http://wwwthebrain.mcgill.ca/flash/d/d_03_p/d_03_p_que/d_03p_que.html
(November 2, 2004).
17 "Choosing Behaviour: The Brain from Top to Bottom," http://www.thebrain
.mcgill.ca/flash/i/i_01_p/d_01_p_que/i_01_p_que.html (March 5, 2005).
18 http://www.brainyquote.com/quote/d/davidogilv161497.html (March 5, 2005).
19 John 20:29 (NIV).
20 Barry Schwartz, "The Tyranny of Choice," *Scientific American*, April 2004,
p. 74.
21 Malcolm Gladwell, *The Tipping Point*, (Boston: Little Brown, 2000), p. 198.
22 Antonio R. Damasio, *Descartes' Error: Emotion, Reason and the Human
Brain*, (New York: Quill, 2000), p. 4.

23 Ibid., p. 7.

24 Ibid., p. 9.

23 Ibid., p. 10.

CHAPTER 5: FAN THE FLAMES

1   Ron Kurtus, "Studying Behavior on Candid Camera," http://www.school-for-champions.com/behavior/candidcamera.htm (November 19, 2000).

2   "Consumers Find Word-of-Mouth Increasingly Important," http://www.cbaonline.org/Conventions/_FOIgoodmind.jsp (April 18, 2005).

3   "Review of the Religious Book Market," *Ipsos BookTrends*, September 2001.

4   "Coal and Charcoal: Blacksmith's Coal, Charcoal and Forges," http://www.anvilfire.com/FAQs/coal.htm (March 7, 2005).

5   http://www.astro.uu.nl/~strous/AA/en/antwoorden/zon.html#v231 (March 7, 2005).

6   Robert B. Cialdini, *Influence: The Psychology of Persuasion* (New York: Quill, 1984), p. 114.

7   Barry Schwartz, "The Tyranny of Choice," *Scientific American*, April 2004, p. 71.

8   Duncan J. Watts, *Six Degrees*, (New York: W. W. Norton, 2003), p. 211.

9   Ibid.

10 Cialdini, p. 116.

11 Philip Yancey, *What's So Amazing About Grace?* visual edition, (Grand Rapids, Michigan: Zondervan, 1997), p. 83.

12 Watts, p. 228.

13 Albert-Lazslo Barabasi, *Linked*, (New York: Plume, 2003), p. 45.

14 Watts, p. 32.

15 Elaine Hatfield, John T. Cacioppo, and Richard L. Rapson, *Emotional Contagion*, (Cambridge, England: Cambridge University Press, 1994).

16 Ibid., p. 11.

17 Ibid., p. 19.

18 Ibid., p. 21.

19 Ibid.

20 Ibid., p. 28.

21 Ibid., p. 169.

22 Ibid., p. 22.

23 Ibid., p. 10.

24 Ibid., p. 15.

25 Malcolm Gladwell, "The Naked Face," http://www.gladwell.com /2002/2002_08_05_a_face.htm (March 7, 2005).

26 Ibid.

27 Ibid.

28 Ibid.

29 Hatfield et al., p. 132.

30 Malcolm Gladwell, *The Tipping Point*, (Boston: Little Brown, 2000), p. 84.

31 Hatfield et al., p. 141.

32 Ibid., p. 143.

33 Ibid., p. 162.

34 Ibid.

35 Ibid., p. 169.

36 http://www.barna.org/FlexPage.aspx?Page=Topic&TopicID=10 (December 12, 2004).

37 Watts, p. 50.

CHAPTER 6: SAVE THE COALS

1 The First 100 Years of Match Making, http://www.matchcovers.com /first100.htm (December 31, 2004).

2 Arthur M. Hughes, *Strategic Database Marketing* (New York: McGraw Hill, 2000), p. 18.

3 Ibid.

4 *Merriam-Webster's Collegiate Dictionary*, 11th ed. (Springfield, Mass.: Merriam-Webster, Inc., 2003).

5 Hughes, p. 105.

6 "Trust Stakes Its Claim to Customer Value," http://www.1to1.com/View.aspx?DocID=28600 (April 18, 2005).

7 Hughes, p. 58.

8 Hughes, p. 18.

9 Cambridge SoundWorks Turns Up the Volume on Its Customers," 1to1@work: database management, http://www.1to1.com/View.aspx ?DocID=28606 (January 29, 2005).

10 Hughes, p. 68.

11 Ibid., p. 16.

12 Cited in Ben McConnell and Jackie Huba, "Creating Customer Communities: A Surgical Approach," http://www.marketingprofs.com /preview.asp?file=/3/mcconhuba1.asp (February 1, 2005).

13 Ibid.

14 http://www.harley-davidson.com/ex/hog/template.asp?locale=en_US
&bmLocate=en_US&fnc=hog (February 1, 2005).

CHAPTER 7: AFTERGLOW

1 Penelope Patsuris, "What Mel's Passion Will Earn Him," *Forbes,* March 3, 2004.

2 Kim Lawton, *Religion and Ethics News Weekly,* January 30, 2004, http://www.pbs.org/wnet/religionandethics/week722/news.html (January 6, 2005).

3 Rosemary Pennington, "Marketing Faith," http://www.wbhm.org/News/2004/Marketing_Faith.html (January 6, 2005).

4 Jeffrey Cobb, "Marketing 'The Passion of the Christ,'" http://www.msnbc.msn.com/id/4374411/ (January 6, 2005).

5 Ibid.

6 Luke 9:20 (NIV).

7 Mark 16:15 (NIV).

8 Acts 1:8 (NIV).

9 http://www.superbowl-ads.com/articles_1999/html_files/BYTOML~1.HTM (January 8, 2005).

10 Albert Einstein, http://www.brainquote.com/quotes/a/alberteins133991.html (April 18, 2005).

11 First published in *Youth's Companion,* vol.76, May 29, 1902, http://sunsite.berkeley.edu/London/Writings/Uncollected/tobuildafire.html, January 4, 2005.